I wish we didn't need this book. Really, I do. I wish the current Christian culture were such that a book like this would be completely superfluous. But it's not. It's needed—desperately needed. As a youth ministry professor at Indiana Wesleyan University, I'm constantly having conversations with young women who want to know, "Could I be a youth pastor too?" I look forward to handing them a copy of Gina's book so they can get current, firsthand information about what it's like to be a woman in the trenches of youth ministry. Gina's conversational style is full of insightful stories and wise tips to help bolster her readers' confidence. While it's true we learn a lot from experience, Gina's vulnerability allows us to learn from her experiences as well. This is a must-read for any young woman who wonders whether God could use her to minister to his children.

**Dr. Amanda Drury**
**Assistant Professor in Practical Theology and Ministry**
**Indiana Wesleyan University**

"It's hard to be awesome when you're too busy." This line from Gina's book rang so true for me. With creativity, honesty, humor, and meaningful advice from her own story, other voices, and God's Word, Gina weaves together a beautiful addition for women in leadership. May we—as individuals and as the church—slow our busyness so the kingdom can be even more awesome.

**April L. Diaz**
**Author of *Redefining the Role of the Youth Worker: A Manifesto for Integration***
**Director of Coaching at The Youth Cartel**
**aprildiaz.com**

W9-CYN-018

The challenge for women in ministry today is not just confronting the overt ways women experience inequality (still very present), but also naming the latent ways inequality is perpetuated in ministries' unchecked assumptions, expressed through programs, postures, relationships, language, and theology. Gina's story is exactly that—a journey packed with encounters, ideas, and questions worth considering. Women and, more importantly, men should read this book and let Gina be another (or maybe their first) female ministry conversation partner.

**Steven Argue**
**Pastor and Theologian-in-Residence, Mars Hill Bible Church**
**Adjunct Professor of Youth Ministries, Grand Rapids**
**Theological Seminary**
**Advisory Council Member, Fuller Youth Institute**

I wish *A Woman in Youth Ministry* had been available when I began my career in youth ministry. I desperately emulated the male youth pastors I knew because I was unsure how to be a woman in youth ministry. This book would have saved me considerable grief and heartache, and enabled me to feel less alone. Gina's stories and wisdom will, no doubt, provide many female youth workers with a road map for how to confidently live into their calling as women in youth ministry. But don't be fooled by the title. This book isn't just for women. It's also for male youth workers who want to partner with their female colleagues more effectively in order to do God's kingdom work.

**Jen Bradbury**
**Director of Youth Ministry, Faith Lutheran Church**
**Author of *The Jesus Gap***

If you're a woman in youth ministry, or know a woman in youth ministry, this book is essential reading. Gina's writing is warm, honest, and encouraging, with a little bit of rear-kicking. I loved how she opened up difficult but essential topics like education, pay, family-life balance, and boundaries. *A Woman in Youth Ministry* is a great resource for women in all levels of youth ministry leadership, from volunteers to youth pastors. You'll return to it over and over.

**Emily Maynard**
**Blogger & Speaker**

I've never read another book like this. *A Woman in Youth Ministry* is a next-level glimpse into the journey of a youth worker—who also happens to be a woman. It's a raw, heartfelt, practical guide to navigating the ups and downs of the youth ministry world. If you're looking for a guide to longevity in youth ministry—you've found it!

**Katie Edwards**
**Saddleback Church**

# A WOMAN
## IN YOUTH MINISTRY

### GINA ABBAS

# A Woman in Youth Ministry

Copyright © 2014 by Gina Abbas

Publisher: Mark Oestreicher
Managing Editor: Laura Gross
Proofreader: Heather Haggerty
Design & Layout: Adam McLane
Creative Director: Priscilla (Romans 16:3)

Scripture quotations marked NIV are taken from THE HOLY BIBLE, NEW INTERNATIONAL VERSION®, NIV® Copyright © 1973, 1978, 1984, 2011 by Biblica, Inc.™ Used by permission. All rights reserved worldwide.

ISBN-13: 978-0-9910050-4-8
ISBN-10: 099100504X

The Youth Cartel, LLC
www.theyouthcartel.com

Email: info@theyouthcartel.com

Born in San Diego
Printed in the U.S.A.

A mi mamá y a mi abuela Julia
Gracias por demostrarme lo que significa ser una mujer fuerte,
amable y llena de gracia.


To Tim
You made countless dinners, moved across the country, put the
kids to bed, and all so I could finish this book and say yes to
being a middle school pastor in Michigan.
I love you.

# CONTENTS

# ACKNOWLEDGMENTS

Thank you Mark Oestreicher and Adam McLane for making this book a reality. I'm also thankful for your relentless support of women in youth ministry.

And thank you Mariah Sherman, Carmen Garrigan, Amanda Drury, Lissa Mann-Cervera, Laura Gross, and the many friends who inspired, supported, and contributed to this project.

# INTRODUCTION

I am a mom. I am a wife. I am a full-time youth ~~worker~~ pastor. Even on the craziest of days when I'm frantically running to and from youth group—sometimes with smashed banana and baby barf in my hair—I love this call to youth ministry. Whether you're single or married, volunteer or paid, youth ministry can be a lifelong calling. You can choreograph a beautiful dance between your life and ministry no matter how busy it gets, how many kids you have (or don't have), or how old you are. If you're 22 or 42 or even 62, you can create space and a rhythm in your week where teenagers, church staff, and ministry colleagues strategically intersect with your everyday life.

And if you're a woman, I want you to know that you can lead a youth ministry and lead it well. You can lead regardless of the varying theological perspectives that exist in regard to women in church leadership. As someone who's experienced some of the best and some of the worst things about being a female in youth ministry, *I hope this book inspires my female readers to lead confidently, love your calling, and lean toward the places and people who value your gifts as a youth worker.*

I am a youth ministry blogger, and almost every single day I get emails and traffic on my blog (http://youthleadergina.blogspot.com/) from women who Google CAN GIRLS BE YOUTH PASTORS? I hope one day this question becomes irrelevant—like it already is for so many of my mainline church friends. But until that day comes, there may be a 15-year-old girl out there somewhere who's like I was back in the late '90s—a girl who needs to see that, yes, women can be youth ministers.

The second most commonly Googled question that sends people to my blog is WHAT CAN YOU DO WITH A YOUTH MINISTRY DEGREE? That one makes me laugh. I have a youth ministry degree. Can't you just picture my parents wondering what the heck I was going to use it for? But I am still using it today as an in-the-trenches, this-has-been-my-life's-calling youth pastor. Sometimes I've been called a "youth director" or a "ministry coordinator," but yeah, I'm a youth pastor.

Have you noticed that books about youth ministry tend to be written by seminary professors or youth ministry experts (authors and conference speakers) who aren't living the youth pastor life seven days a week like the rest of us? Most of these authors don't receive angry phone calls from parents or do hourly head counts on a bus trip to somewhere. They don't have to think up games, scramble for small group leaders, run campus clubs, or pick curriculum for the next school year. And another drawback to many of the books about youth ministry today is that most of the authors are men. I want to read a book about being a female youth pastor that was actually written by a female youth pastor. So when I couldn't find a recent one, I decided to write one instead.

Women email me daily asking for my help on finding other women in youth ministry for them to connect with or wanting me to mentor them. I hope that reading this book will be a lot like having me mentor you. Just pretend we're sitting together at a local coffee shop (FAR away from your church so you don't have to worry about anyone overhearing our conversation), and let's get real together. I'll share my stories—the good ones and the difficult ones—and answer many of the questions that women in youth ministry often ask me.

If you're a guy reading this book, then I just have to say: Wow! The girls in youth ministry are going to love you! You, dear brother, are going to get an inside look at what's it like for women serving in youth ministry. And as you grow in your understanding of the challenges female youth pastors face, your leadership abilities will also grow. As I share my advice, tips, and wisdom from more than a decade of youth ministry, I know you will glean some helpful insights and leadership tips too.

This book offers a sneak peek into those challenging days of juggling ministry, marriage, and motherhood. It's like my very own behind-the-scenes look at the struggles and triumphs of sticking with the beautiful, messy, challenging call of ministering to teenagers. I've been doing this youth ministry thing since I was a single woman in my 20s. Now I'm an almost-40-year-old mom of three working full time as a middle school pastor. Some days have been full of wow and wonder as I've seen God do some pretty amazing stuff in the lives of teenagers. Other days I want to quit and go work at Target.

I know what it's like to run a youth ministry in both large and small churches. I've worked in super conservative environments and in more liberal to moderate ones too. I've worked where booze was banned and where I was served margaritas out of a gas can. (Woot woot, Presbys!) You probably have similar stories you could share. So let's get this conversation started.

# 1

# YOUTH PASTORS CAN BE GIRLS? WHY DIDN'T ANYONE TELL ME?!

While walking with my husband through the vendor exhibit hall at several national youth ministry conferences over the years, I've found one thing to be true: Everyone thinks my husband is the youth pastor. They look him in the eye and try to get him to sign up for their youth mission trips or summer camps. He just grins and looks at me as he playfully introduces himself as "the pastor's wife." Then I step forward to grab the brochure and a Tootsie Pop, and lay claim to yet another free, oversized T-shirt. I now have about 50 of these youth ministry–themed T-shirts that only fit my husband. (Apparently these companies believe only large men do youth ministry.) But women in youth ministry are no strangers to this assumption that many people, primarily in conservative Protestant evangelical churches, seem to have that all youth pastors are men.

My daughter Jenna walked into the kitchen one morning while I was pouring her a bowl of Cinnamon Toast Crunch. With a look of concern, she said, "Mom, my friends said girls can't be youth pastors." Clearly this is a hot topic if even second graders are discussing it on the playground.

I looked into her curious, bright blue eyes and said, "Well, *I'm* a youth pastor. Am I a girl?"

She replied with a smile and a nod, answering me with a big "Duhhh!" as a little bit of the milk from her cereal bowl ran off her spoon and down her chin.

After pausing for a moment, I asked, "Do you remember Anna, the girl with curly hair in first grade? Guess what her mom is." She looked blankly at me as she tried to remember Anna. I reminded her, "You know, my friend Tina's daughter. Well, Anna's mom is a youth pastor too, and *she's* a girl." I could see Jenna connecting the dots.

As we continued our chat over our bowls of cereal, I said, "My friend Carmen, do you know what she is?"

Jenna replied, "A youth pastor!" She smiled from ear to ear.

Taking a sip of my coffee, I asked, "You know Caitlin in Josh's fifth grade class? She belongs to my friend Christina, and guess what...she's a youth pastor too. And what about Mariah?" (One of Jenna's favorite people.) "Can you tell me what she does?"

"She is a youth pastor!" Jenna said with a giddy squeal.

"So, Jenna, can girls be youth pastors?" I asked.

She looked at me eyeball to eyeball and said, "YES!"

I am so thankful to live and serve in a community with so many female youth pastors and youth ministry volunteers around. Three of us youth ministry women have kids in the same public elementary school. I'm blessed to have many friends who serve as real-life examples to my eight-year-old daughter of women serving as youth pastors (or "coordinators" or "directors" or "volunteer youth ministers" or whatever the title may be)!

## IT'S MY NORMAL

I grew up in a congregation where we had a female pastor until I was 15. Since that was my normal, I never knew it wasn't everyone's normal until I went to college. During college I heard God's call to ministry; I knew seminary would be the next step for me. When I told people my plan, the professors I admired most were supportive of me, but I did get a few looks from other students—like I had five heads or something. It never daunted me though because I had my college church and my home church's support 100 percent, and my sense of call was never questioned because of my gender.

Currently I'm serving in a youth ministry position at a church led by a female head pastor. Since female leadership has been such a significant part of my discipleship process with my students, my challenge is to make sure I provide plenty of godly male role models in their lives so they don't think ministry and preaching is only "women's work."

— *Carmen Garrigan*

If girls aren't meant to be youth pastors, then I guess a lot of us didn't get that memo. If you want to be a woman in youth ministry, clearly there *are* churches that have both men and women in leadership positions who *do* hire women for youth ministry positions. And some of them might even call you a "pastor."

When I think of my daughters and the teenage girls in my own youth group, I can't help but wonder about the limitations some churches and institutions put on women. I understand the well-meaning desire of trying to be faithful to Scripture. There are many well-executed arguments for and against women serving in church leadership. And I am well versed in complementarian theology. I took that class in Bible college. A conservative, evangelical white male taught it. Having been told by male Bible teachers and supervisors how women and men are equal but created for different roles, I leaned into every role that was given to me. Girl Intern. Girl Camp Counselor. Youth Ministry Coordinator. Giving it my best.

But the more I lived into my gender-based "acceptable role" in youth ministry, the more I saw the limitations it placed on gifted women and the damage it did to the relationships between the men and women who were working together in ministry. I wondered and asked if evangelical Christianity was sending an anti-women message. Cedarville University in Ohio, a large private Christian college, made news recently because they have "restricted classes in the women's ministry program—functionally, every Bible class in the fall schedule taught by a woman—to only female students, according to alumni and a university representative"[1] When our daughters and sons are exposed to only male Bible teachers, and when female Bible teachers are restricted by gender—everyone loses. What message are we speaking into the future of those who come home from second grade asking, "Mom, can girls be youth pastors?"

I want my own children to have an expanded view of limitless ministry and Bible-teaching opportunities. Opportunities to use their gifts and learn from each other without gender limitations. We must surround our sons and daughters with an empowering ability to imagine, hear, and discern a call to pastoral ministry. To see men and women, brothers and sisters in Christ, working together to make a difference as they build God's kingdom and bring hope, faith, and love into the world through the redeeming work of Jesus Christ—not sitting on separate sides of the room or being forced to drive in separate cars.

I didn't grow up knowing that girls can be youth pastors or Bible teachers. I grew up in a small youth ministry led by guys. I can't even remember any females helping out too often. If they did, the single guy youth workers and male volunteers probably kept hitting on them and scared them away. The only women I ever saw on church staff were church secretaries and piano players. That is, until I met Lissa on my first day of high school.

I'd flown under the radar during middle school, having never been Miss Popular nor voted "best dressed" or "class clown" by my classmates. So I saw my high school years as my chance to change all of that. I was determined to chart a new course, to do whatever it took to "be cool." So it was my first day of high school and *finally* my chance to be whomever I wanted to be had arrived. And then Lissa walked over to me during lunch period. She was a really short girl who looked 11 years old. She had fluffy curly brown hair, a round face, and bright pink cheeks. She was wearing no makeup, pink sweatpants, a pink sweatshirt, and white tennis shoes; and she was holding a lunchbox. Can you imagine my internal dilemma when, gripping her lunchbox tightly, Lissa timidly asked to join my lunch table?

I briefly thought about saying no and sending her on her way. I *really* wanted to be cool—and Lissa was so not cool. I mean, she looked more like a Care Bear than a ninth grader. And who brings a lunchbox to high school? You'd have thought it was the first day of sixth grade, not freshman year. But at that moment I gave up any attempt at coolness and decided I'd rather choose kindness. It felt better to my soul. And looking back on it now, I know that no one at that lunch table was ever going to be cool anyway.

I grew up in a Christian family, but it was during lunch period on that first day of high school that my faith became my own. While sitting at a table surrounded by green grass, palm trees, and perfect Southern California weather, I decided it was better to follow Jesus. Being "cool" just didn't seem worth it if it meant I had to hurt people. Living a life of love and grace became something I chose for myself. Except, I went to the other extreme.

Apparently, I'm an all-or-nothing kind of person. I became president of the Christian club at school, signed up to be a student leader in my church youth group, and made my friend Heather cry at lunch one day because I tried to pressure her to accept Jesus so she wouldn't go to hell. (I was kind of immature when it came to evangelism.) My longtime friend Mark, who'd been crushing on me since middle school, was my senior prom date because my super-cute, college-aged boyfriend had dumped me because I didn't like him touching my boobs. Basically, I left my mark on high school by being voted "Most likely to become a nun." And so there I was at my prom with Mark who'd been voted "Most likely to become a priest." You could say I wasn't cool—not even a little bit.

Nevertheless, I loved ministry. I loved people and I felt a tug, a calling, and a giftedness toward preaching; yet I had no idea what to do with that. I'd never seen girls preach or lead in the churches I'd attended growing up. But when I was 15, all of that changed. Lissa (who by now had started dressing more like a high schooler and less like a stuffed animal) invited me to her youth group. It was my first time inside a Catholic church. Going to Lissa's youth group was fun, and of course I was a typical ninth grader asking, "What games are we gonna play?" The youth group was similar to mine in some ways, but it was also quite a bit different. Her church hosted several youth dances, and alcohol was allowed (for the grownups) at their annual all-church street festival. Her Jesus-loving church was a lot different than my Jesus-loving church. And I *loved* it.

That's where I met Lissa's youth director, Barbara Brown—the first female youth pastor I'd ever met. She was a mom of high school kids, so she was older than my hip, somewhere-in-his-twenties youth pastor. And there in the parish hall of Holy Trinity Catholic Church in El Cajon, California, while jumping and singing along to "Kriss Kross'll make ya...jump! Jump!" with a pack of sweaty teens is *where I first realized youth pastors can be girls*. Why didn't anyone ever tell me this? It changed the trajectory of my life. At that moment my view of women in ministry expanded beyond my own conservative evangelical Protestant worldview. It was a game changer. And my friend Lissa has been pulling me forward into new and better ways of thinking and loving ever since. You mean, "Youth pastors can be *girls*?" Yup.

So yeah, the church can call us "directors," "coordinators," "pastors," or whatever title they prefer. But never forget that whether you're paid, volunteer, or bivocational; whether you're single or married, *God can use you* as a woman in youth ministry. Maybe you're like Lissa, where seeing women serving in youth ministry is a no-brainer. It's all you've known. Perhaps you had a female youth pastor or you grew up not knowing that gender was an issue in ministry. If so, then you obviously don't carry Southern Baptist baggage like I do. Or maybe, like me, you learned from someone a little later in life, like a Barbara or a Lissa, that youth workers can be male or female.

I realize there is a wide spectrum of opinions and biblical interpretations regarding women in ministry leadership, but this isn't a book about that. I'm not trying to change anyone's mind. However, I do want to share my youth ministry journey and pose questions for others to ponder regarding their own calling within their own theological framework. If you aren't sure about your theological view of women in church leadership, it's definitely something you need to wrestle with. There are three main views: hierarchical, complementarian, and egalitarian. You can read a brief description of each of the three below:

**Egalitarian**—This view sees women and men as equal in both the home and in the church. Both men and women are able to use their gifts in any capacity or office of the church. Gender is not in and of itself a disqualification or reason to limit ministry opportunities.

**Complementarian**—This is a view that sees women and men as equal, but serving in different complementary roles both within the church and in the home. Complementary theology typically sees women's roles as those supporting men, while advocating that they are an equal and important part of church leadership.

**Hierarchical**—This is a view that sees women as subordinate to men both in the home and in the church. It's similar to the complementarian view, but much more of an emphasis on male headship and patriarchy. This view restricts women to little more than ministry to other women and children within the church.

It's really important to know your own hermeneutic regarding women in leadership, as well as that of the church where you work or volunteer. Theology shapes your day-to-day experience and will impact your opportunities and expectations as a woman in youth ministry. But whatever context you're in and however you lean theologically, you must confidently embrace your calling as a woman in youth ministry. Serve and work in the places and with the people who allow you to be you in all of your giftedness.

Women in conservative evangelical churches and colleges often ask me, "Can I lead as a female in youth ministry?" For better or worse, many churches don't consider leading a youth group to be quite the same thing as leading adults. In many youth ministry paradigms, an age-specific church program for teens is simply the next logical step after they graduate from the children's ministry. Sadly, some in senior church leadership positions (thankfully, not all) view a church youth group as little more than a donut-and-Mountain-Dew–filled holding tank for pre-teens and teens until they reach adulthood—with some Jesus, summer camps, mission trips, decision cards, and confirmation classes tossed in, of course. And because youth ministry positions aren't considered "senior leadership"

## THE IMPORTANCE OF TEAM MINISTRY

A few years ago, I decided to keep a running tally of every issue that was brought to me by a female student. As you can imagine, these girls could not (and should not) address these issues with their male youth pastor. God created teenage girls to be unique. They have their own emotions, temptations, desires, and needs. And I was extremely fortunate to work in a situation where I was blessed with male coworkers who humbly let me shine in the areas where they could not. Female youth pastors need to be given the space to use their unique and God-given gifts well.

During my youth ministry career, I've heard statements like, "Thank you for showing our daughter what a healthy marriage looks like," and "Thank you for consistently showing our daughters what dressing modestly looks like." These are the kinds of things that male youth pastors simply can't teach their female students. And it's not because they're bad at their jobs or because they don't have a desire to mentor female students. There are just some areas of a girl's life that only another woman can speak in to.

Female students need more than a ministry that centers around dodgeball tournaments and side hugs. Female students need a ministry where they can see female role models who serve as good examples of a life spent chasing after God.

— *Angie Williamson*

or executive staff, conservative evangelical churches with a complementarian/hierarchical hermeneutic for figuring out gender roles in ministry do welcome women to serve and lead in youth ministry.

Churches from complementarian theological perspectives are hiring women and recruiting female volunteers to oversee youth ministry small groups, girls' ministry, campus ministry, curriculum development, or to work on staff as an assistant youth pastor with a male youth pastor as the lead. Women with a hierarchical or complementarian theological view of women in ministry are likely to work mostly or even exclusively with teenagers and staff of their own gender, and there is no shortage of ministry opportunities to do so. And if your church is egalitarian in its theology, well then you're probably already leading your own youth ministry without any gender limitations and are enjoying much more equality in ministry than many of your sisters in Christ do.

So my answer to the question "Can I lead as a female in youth ministry?" is women can and do lead in all kinds of youth ministry settings, with varying titles and many different types of roles.

As I touched on before, in a majority of churches the youth ministry falls under the children's and youth ministry departments; therefore, it allows—and needs—both men and women to serve on these teams. Usually there is a Christian education director, educational pastor, or associate pastor of some kind overseeing the teen and children's ministries. This is especially true in larger churches. It's also true in churches that haven't yet adopted or intentionally integrated their teenagers and kids into the life and rhythm of the church at large, and still keep tons of separate programming going.

Many churches need a large and diverse youth ministry staff. The need for men and women to lead, volunteer, and pastor male and female teenagers still exists in every kind of church everywhere. Even in the conservative Southern Baptist churches I have known and loved, they always had an awareness of the need to have women on their youth ministry team. If you are called to youth ministry, you are going to find a way to serve and love on teenagers. Look around. There are women in youth ministry everywhere.

Maybe there is a 15-year-old girl like me who needs to see that she can be a youth pastor. Will you lead the charge to show our girls and boys and conservative evangelical friends that there are plenty of women, paid and unpaid, serving in youth ministry? Will you step outside of your denominational networks and mix it up with others from different perspectives so they can see what you already know to be true? For many of you, women serving in youth ministry was never a question, never an issue—you've always known that #GirlsCan—and others need to hear that.

# QUESTIONS FOR REFLECTION

1. Did you always know that women can be youth workers? What was your experience of and/or exposure to women doing youth ministry?

2. What denominational affiliation did you grow up in (or not) and how has that shaped your view of women in ministry?

3. When did you first sense a call to serve as a paid or volunteer youth worker?

4. Is there a particular person who inspired you to want to serve in youth ministry?

5. Did you already know about the three theological views of women in church leadership?

6. What is your view of women in ministry? Is it the same or different than the church where you serve now or the church you grew up in?

7. If you are or were a Bible college or seminary student, what is the view of women in ministry at that educational institution?

8. How does your theology of women in leadership and gender roles in marriage inform and influence your ministry, your relationships, and your expectations?

# 2

# BOSSY BRITTANY

Women are serving and leading in youth ministry. They're interning. Volunteering. Pastoring. Here's a question I want you to ponder for a moment: *Regardless of your context, when you have opportunities to lead as a woman in youth ministry, do you?* Like most good youth leaders, I read the book *Divergent*. One of my favorite parts is when Tris first gets to the Dauntless headquarters. Before going in, Max, a Dauntless leader, tells the new crowd of initiates that several stories below them is the entrance to the compound. If they don't have the courage to jump, they don't belong in the Dauntless faction. As new initiates they get to jump first.

> *No one looks eager to leap off the building—their eyes are everywhere but on Max.*[2]

Tris makes her way to the front and jumps first. Before the boys. Before the other girls. When everyone else avoids eye contact, she leads.

I've spent the majority of my youth ministry career working with a lot of paid staff, volunteers, and interns. And working on a large ministry staff revealed to me a variety of personality types and leadership styles. What I noticed is that certain personality types always rise to the surface as leaders—regardless of their position or gender.

Brittany, a female youth leader who worked in our youth group snack bar (at a church where only men could be pastors), was one of the more vocal leaders on our team. She had more leadership giftedness and raw senior leadership potential than many of our full-time paid pastors. Paid or unpaid, intern or pastor, volunteer or veteran youth worker, male or female… leaders lead. And if a zombie apocalypse ever comes to fruition or if I should get stranded on an island as a contestant on *Survivor*, I want Brittany with me. She can command a room, lead people to safety during a crisis, and confidently pave the way to anywhere! She's someone you naturally want to follow. What's ironic is she now attends a church in the Pacific Northwest that's led by a well-known pastor who's been very vocal about how he's *against* women serving in ministry leadership roles. Even so, I'm pretty confident Brittany will continue to lead in whatever environment she's in.

A guy Brittany and I worked with once told me he thought Brittany was bossy, but I knew she was simply leading and leading well. He was threatened by her confidence, and he tried to hide his insecurity behind the label he gave her: "Bossy Brittany." Strong female leaders like Brittany are often (unfairly) labeled as "bossy." And it's easy to spot the double standard when those same traits are deemed as "leadership qualities" in men. Facebook's COO Sheryl Sandberg addresses this issue in her book *Lean In*:

> *"We call our little girls bossy," Sandberg says. "Go to a playground: Little girls get called 'bossy' all the time, a word that's almost never used for boys. And that leads directly to the problems women face in the workforce. When a man does a good job, everyone says, 'That's great.' When a woman does that same thing, she'll get feedback that says things like, 'Your results are good,*

*but your peers just don't like you as much' or 'maybe you were a little aggressive.' "[3]*

Taking inspiration from Sheryl's book, the Girl Scouts jumped on board and launched a "Ban Bossy" campaign to empower girls to lead. And Pantene created a moving and eye-opening video called "Labels Against Women" as part of their #ShineStrong campaign in the Philippines.[4] As the video ends, it urges women not to let labels hold them back. Not surprisingly, it went viral and received a big thumbs up from Sandberg.

Generally speaking, women who get labeled as "the bossy ones" are the Lions on Gary Smalley and John Trent's personality types inventory,[5] they're extroverts, they're 8s on the Enneagram,[6] or they're ENTJs on the Myers-Briggs assessment.[7] If you aren't familiar with these kinds of character trait inventories or personality profiles, I highly suggest them to you. They're wonderful tools for figuring out what drives you and the people you work with. You can learn a lot about your leadership style from these kinds of things. Yet, regardless of which personality inventory you've taken online or even if

## GOOD LEADERSHIP OR BAD MANNERS?

In 2007, the executive staff at my church asked everyone to complete an evaluation. One of the questions was, "What was your worst day at work in the last year?" Much to their surprise, I listed an exact date: March 16. That was the day my boss, a male, called me into his office and then called me "abrasive." He did so because I'd refused to give in on issues that were important to me. According to him, this was disrespectful.

I, on the other hand, thought it was leadership. Such is the peril of being a woman in ministry. What we think is strong leadership, others view as bad manners.

— *Jen Bradbury*

it was just a cheesy "What's Your Leadership Style?" quiz in *Seventeen Magazine*, the fact remains: There are people who are leaders, and there are people who are not.

Even if you're occasionally labeled as bossy or whenever you find yourself involved in conflict with others on staff, you still must lead and lead well. What creates problems and hinders leadership opportunities for women isn't necessarily a lack of opportunity, but a lack of willingness to grab or demand or sometimes even sneak a seat at the ministry table. In really conservative (male-dominated) evangelical circles that hold a very narrow hierarchical or complementarian theological view of women in ministry, leaders still always find a way to lead.

Keep leading. Perhaps your specific ministry context limits your leadership from the top down. Look for ways to lead up, lead out, and lead the way within whatever context you're in. Even when Brittany got called bossy or wasn't given the final say in ministry leadership decisions, she never shrank back from being a leader. She carefully navigated the waters of being in charge without really "being the person in charge." You can pay a leader, but you can't create one.

A strong Type A, extroverted, confident female who works or volunteers in a conservative evangelical environment that leans heavily toward supporting only men in leadership roles might feel frustrated by leadership limitations. Lead anyway. Whether you're leading from the top as the paid youth pastor in a mainline church environment, or leading as a volunteer girls' small group leader, look for ways to influence the areas of the church and youth ministry in which you're already leading. When placed in charge of a weekend retreat or asked to plan the next youth Sunday, step up and lead confidently. Give it 100 percent.

When it comes to leading, recent studies show that confidence is the key to being taken seriously. Claire Shipman, coauthor of

*The Confidence Code: The Science and Art of Self-Assurance—
What Women Should Know*, shares: "People who are actually
not just confident, but slightly overconfident, do better. They
get more success, they're viewed as leaders of the pack, and
their ideas carry more weight."[8]

Brittany was a confident leader and it showed. She'd be put
in charge when other leaders were absent. She was asked to
help lead mission trips, teach on occasion, and if the in-charge
pastor were ever to leave the room, there was never a worry
about things getting out of hand if Brittany was there. She had
the confidence, charm, and people skills to lead—and lead she
did. Her ideas carried weight because she wasn't afraid to share
them.

I worked for several years in a church under hierarchical
complementarian leadership. The combination of the church's
theology limiting the leadership of women and my drive to lead
created a lot of challenges that I admit I could have navigated
better. Had I been more tuned in to my supervisor's (and my
own) leadership style, personality, and theological motivation, I
would have had a better framework for discerning my call into

## DRILL SERGEANT

A man whom I thought I knew decently enough was volunteering
during some youth ministry activities. He commented to me,
while others were within earshot, that I'm "like a drill sergeant"
and noted he's "a little bit scared of me." Now, you don't know
me, but I am in no way drill sergeant-esque, nor am I scary. I'm
mostly quiet. I'm not physically intimidating. I tend to lead by
empowering others. I'm in the background more than I am in
the foreground. However, I can also command the attention of
a room full of people and quickly delegate and facilitate work
getting done when that's what I need to do. When he said I was
like a drill sergeant, I wondered, *Would he have said that to a
man? Or would he have just thought the man was taking charge?*
— *Heather Henderson*

that kind of a ministry environment. So my advice is don't take on a ministry role or volunteer position that ends up being the equivalent of signing up to play baseball without ever being allowed to bat. It's a disappointment I could have avoided if I'd spent more time discerning my own theology and leadership style. But I was never taught how to do that in Bible college, nor did a ministry mentor ever talk me through the process.

You must take the time to discern if your challenges, conflicts, disappointments, or lack of opportunity in ministry are based on theology, personality, or gender differences (sometimes all of the above). Have you heard the phrase "too many cooks in the kitchen"? It's an overused old saying, but you get the picture. A heated situation arises when too many leaders are fighting for their own ideas or ministry areas. Or another good example is trying to plan a wedding with two strong, opinionated mothers and some sisters in the mix. The problem is when you're a female who's trying to lead and you work with a lot of males, there is the ugly reality that you may get called bossy—or even bitchy.

Ezra Klein, editor-in-chief of *Vox.com*, interviewed Claire Shipman for an article titled "Competent Women Are Getting Bypassed by Overconfident Men." In that interview, Ezra said, "There are a lot of manifestations of confidence that, when men put them forward, are considered to be very attractive, and when women put them forward, to just be blunt about it, the women are then spoken about behind their backs as a "bitch."[9] The fact that Brittany was being called bossy behind her back was proof to me that she is a confident leader. Not a bitch. Not at all.

Female leaders need to discern when it's time to step back and learn how to be a part of a healthy team, but they also need the courage to take the leap, lead others, and advocate for their ministry. Whether it's planning for a youth ministry event or planning your wedding day, don't be afraid to step into your

## LEAD WITH A BEAUTY THAT IS BOLD, NOT BOSSY

In order to lead well as a woman in ministry, you have to learn to be secure in your identity as a minister. This isn't always easy to do as a woman; we thrive on the affirmation we receive from pleasing others. But as you know, 90 percent of the emails in your mailbox aren't letters of encouragement, but requests and feedback and junk mail. We have to learn how to receive critique in a way that doesn't tie it to our personal identities. This translates to not only how we receive communication, but how we give it as well.

I have personally struggled with overcompensating for my lack of confidence by trading it for a false arrogance. Of course, when a female leads with pride, she becomes a nag, a manipulator, or a "female dog." Therefore, I need to trade my lack of self-confidence for the image of God who says to me, "I have created you to lead with a beauty that is bold and not bossy; a strength that is secure and not sassy; a valor that is vibrant and not vindictive." Leading with courage and assurance will be contagious to everyone who watches you lead. Trust me—this is why *I* look to the women who lead me.

— *Heather Lea Campbell*

leadership gifts and follow your vision. Play nice. Be a team player and empower others. Of course, you should be gracious and take time to advocate for what others in your ministry are passionate about too. It's vital to set aside your own agenda at times and purposefully seek where God is leading and working within your youth ministry. It's not being bossy to follow God's lead and be a champion for the best way to love and serve youth.

You should seek to work or volunteer in a youth ministry setting that allows you to be true to your theology, the church's theology (of women in ministry leadership), and your giftedness for leading others. Are you comfortable with the capacity in which you're allowed to lead in your particular setting? "Bossy Brittany" led because she was able to lead within a theological framework she agreed with. She was completely comfortable serving under hierarchical complementarian leadership. She may not have run the ministry, but she ran that snack bar and her girls' small group darn well. Brittany admirably led people in a youth ministry she loved. What more could she ask for?

So if someone calls you bossy, take it as a compliment. Congratulations! You're probably a great leader!

# QUESTIONS FOR REFLECTION

1. Have you ever taken any type of personality or leadership inventory? What did you discover about yourself and those you work with?

2. Go on YouTube and watch the video "Labels Against Women" from Pantene's #ShineStrong campaign. What do you think of it?

3. How might it be helpful to discern when conflict in ministry is a personality clash or a leadership style clash?

4. Has there ever been a time when you took initiative and led the way? What happened? What would you do differently if you had to do it all over again?

5. Are you an introvert or an extrovert? How does this impact or influence your leadership?

6. What are some tips you might share for leading others while still being faithful to how God designed your unique personality and leadership style?

7. Are you comfortable with the capacity in which you're allowed to lead in your particular setting?

8. How would you handle being called "bossy"?

# 3

# THE MIDDLE SCHOOL DANCE

As a middle school pastor, I've had the opportunity to chaperone several awkward yet memorable middle school dances where a hip, tattooed DJ facilitates an energetic abundance of loud music, and moms sell snacks at the back of the gym. At every middle school dance, there is always a guys' side and a girls' side. Occasionally a brave middle school girl who looks like a high school junior will be spotted slow dancing with a much shorter boy who hasn't hit his growth spurt yet. But this happens only on that rare occasion when the DJ plays a boring love ballad. (You know the ones I'm talking about.) I may spot one or two "couples" in the crowd, but 95 percent of the middle school student body tends to stay far away from "the other side" of the gym. Boys on one side. Girls on the other.

When I'm at a ministry meeting, event, or lunch where the rest of the group is mostly men, I've noticed a return to those middle school dynamics. The few women who are present will gravitate toward the familiar (as do the men) and sit near each other, thereby creating a "girls' side" and a "boys' side" at almost every church leadership gathering I've ever been to. And if there is a Q&A time or an invitation for someone from the group to close in prayer, more often than not the women are hesitant to volunteer to pray or step up and ask a question.

I attended an event at a local seminary where a prominent New Testament scholar was invited to speak. I sat in on one session where the room was mostly filled with male seminary students and local pastors, but there were a fair number of female attendees as well. What baffled me was that when the time came for the speaker to take questions from the audience, not a single female was brave enough to ask a question. Including me. The next time you're in a meeting, but particularly one with a mixed group of people who don't know each other too well, observe the women. Do they "lead with gusto,"[10] or do they shrink back in silence?

Middle school dances make me think of a book I read nearly a decade ago called *Just Walk Across the Room* by Bill Hybels. This book placed a powerful image in my head about initiative, courage, and the simple power of walking across a room. The author was talking about evangelism; I use it as a mental image for leadership. I currently work at a progressive church with an egalitarian hermeneutic for understanding the role of women in leadership, and there is no glass ceiling. But even so, it's easy to forget to step into the voice that I'm allowed to have there. It's easy to enter a room and just let the guys speak up.

I took this position after working at a church where the men wore ties and went to executive staff meetings. The guys were called pastors. Women were "coordinators." So I was used to a culture of male-only private gatherings of the senior leadership, where women took notes and brought coffee. I wasn't used to having a seat at the table.

Last week we had a training dinner for our youth ministry volunteers. There was an overabundance of food. We ordered way too much. Why does youth ministry always involve so much food? This overabundance resulted in a staff-wide email being sent out the next morning, inviting everyone to make their way to the church kitchen and grab some leftovers for lunch. So around 11 a.m., I walked over to the kitchen because my lunch of one granola bar wasn't cutting it.

As I rounded the corner, I saw our church's teaching pastor standing in the kitchen—and I turned right around. I'm an introvert but that's not the whole story. In my last ministry position at a megachurch in Southern California, I was never allowed such close proximity and easy access to the teaching pastor due to some Southern Baptist patriarchal hierarchical staff dynamics. There'd always been a bodyguard, a special parking space, a faraway office, a staff pastor, and an executive secretary standing between the celebrity teaching pastor and the rest of us lower-level staff.

It's not that way at my current church, but I wasn't used to it yet. Plus, the teaching pastor is the 37-year-old popular one with a vibe of "cool," while I'm the 37-year-old unknown newbie on staff. Basically, I felt like the awkward little sister. After five seconds of wimpiness, I turned around again and reminded myself that I was allowed a seat at the table, and this wasn't a time to be wimpy but confident. Remember, leaders *lead*, right?

I walked into the kitchen and said, "Hey, welcome back!" (He'd just returned from leading a group of people to the Holy Land.) He said hello and asked what all the food was from. "Oh, we had youth group last night with a leader training time afterward. Apparently we ordered too much food." I mentioned something about his daughter being at youth group. (Turns out she wasn't there. It was a different Lucy with long brown hair. Oops.) He asked how my job was going. I said, "Good." And then I told him how my husband and I had just bought a house and how awesome the housing prices are in Grand Rapids compared to Southern California. That was pretty much the gist of it. It was a two-minute conversation that never would have happened in the patriarchal megachurch world I know so well.

Whether it's in youth ministry or in business, women need to lead with confidence. As women in youth ministry, we must step up and move toward the people, places, and opportunities that allow women to lead and to lead well. We must take initiative and speak up. Last week I attended a local youth ministry network meeting, a casual gathering of male and female youth workers from the surrounding community. At the end, the male youth pastor who'd led this particular meeting asked if someone wanted to close in prayer. I waited, wondering if any of the women would speak up.

*Silence. Not a single female volunteered.*

I get the whole "I'm an introvert—please don't ask me to pray out loud" thing. But when women are given a chance to lead or an opportunity to speak up, we need to shrug off our insecurities and lead—and lead *well*.

Sometimes leading means taking an uncomfortable walk across a room. We had an all-staff Thanksgiving lunch at my current church. As the staff began to arrive, everyone stood closest to the people they were most familiar and comfortable with. I noticed all of the female staff were chatting on one side of the room (and in a church that champions equality!), and all of the men were way over on the other side of the room. It was almost as though an invisible line existed between us. I joked, "Hey, this isn't middle school," and I walked over to the guys' side of the room and engaged in conversation with them. I had to be intentional about it, and I had to leave my "introvert bubble" in order to purposefully embrace the equality that was available to me. I was not going to wimp out and stay in familiar territory. After all, I'd moved from San Diego to Michigan to get that equality. Why hide out now?

When we finally sat down to eat, men sat with women.

Executive staff mingled and partook in a meal with ministry staff. No divas. No bodyguards. It felt natural. It was normal. It was *fun*. We joined together as brothers and sisters. It gave me hope that all churches can move forward in equality not only when it comes to gender, but also position. One person may be the "face" of the church and write the best-selling books, but we're all on the same team. Moving forward into something beautiful. Something better than before. Giving men and women a place to lead together and to lead well, regardless of gender or personality type.

Leading well as a woman in ministry also means thinking twice before you volunteer to be the designated secretary or note taker—not out of arrogance, but for the sake of creating greater awareness. Within the last two weeks, I took part in two different Protestant evangelical gatherings. One was a conference call of youth leaders from across the country, and the other was a meeting of a local youth worker network. At both gatherings, men asked women to "Please write this down" or edit documents. These women are co-laborers in the field of youth ministry, not administrative assistants. I'm all for collaboration and teamwork, and I'm not above taking notes now and then. But even so, I wish men weren't so quick to choose women to be the designated secretary. It's not because I'm snobby or think I'm all that. It's because I want to help men reframe the way they treat women in ministry. If you're a male in ministry, please think twice before you ask your female staff to be the note takers. Think about what message you're sending.

A middle school pastor I worked with on staff once gave me a Starbucks gift card on Administrative Professionals' Day. It was a nice gesture, I suppose, but I led that youth ministry *with him*. I wasn't his or anyone else's admin. Sometimes the men we work or volunteer with in youth ministry are oblivious to how their words, actions, and assumptions impact us. So instead of walking away mad and disgruntled, name it. Tell them how it makes you feel. Say, "Hey, thanks for the Starbucks card. But the last time I checked my job description, it didn't say I was your admin."

Men won't improve the way they treat us if we pretend everything's fine when it's not. Staying silent when we feel wronged will only perpetuate unhealthy work relationships. They may have no idea how we interpret their actions. A male colleague of mine took me to lunch one day and said, "I probably do some dumb, knuckleheaded things. If I ever offend you or do something degrading toward women in ministry, please tell me." I have so much respect for this guy. I was impressed by his desire for accountability.

While on a flight from Grand Rapids to Cincinnati, I overheard a conversation between one of the flight attendants and a female passenger in her mid-50s who was sitting in the emergency exit row. I guessed the woman was a teacher since she was grading a stack of papers. She appeared healthy, strong, and not at all frail or feeble. But when the flight attendant asked the woman if she'd be okay assisting other passengers in the event of an emergency, she kindly declined and asked for another seat on the plane. The flight attendant said:

> *"I'll ask a man to trade seats with you. They're usually willing."*

At that moment I wanted to speak up and say to this teacher on behalf of her students, on behalf of all women, and on behalf of herself, "You can handle this! Step up to any opportunity to lead and lead well! Don't wimp out!"

The flight attendant then asked a tall, strong-looking gentleman a few rows back to trade seats with the teacher. And as the woman passed me and took her new seat, she mumbled apologetically, "I don't like flying."

As I thought some more about that brief preflight exchange, I wanted to advise the flight attendant—on behalf of womankind—to refrain from saying, "I'll ask a man." Instead, perhaps she could say, "I'll find another willing person." Let's not perpetuate the damaging image of weak and frail women who can't handle assisting others in case of an emergency.

Like that teacher, we may feel afraid to speak up. Pray out loud. Raise our hand. Take a seat at the table. Maybe it's due to our personality. We might be introverts. Maybe we're shy. Many of us struggle with fears and insecurities. But instead of cowering, we must be strong. When you have opportunities to lead or to walk into a church kitchen and have a conversation with the teaching pastor, don't wimp out. Lead and do it well.

# QUESTIONS FOR REFLECTION

1. Has leading as a female in youth ministry ever felt like attending an awkward middle school dance? Why or why not?

2. Consider a time when you had a chance to lead or stay silent. How did it turn out?

3. Have you watched women in your life lead well? What did they do? What did you learn from them?

4. Observe: The next time you're in a mixed group and someone asks, "Does anyone want to pray?" see if any women volunteer.

5. Have you ever had to confront a male staff member or pastor for treating you like an administrative assistant? What happened? Would you do it again?

6. Name something in this chapter on leading that challenged you. What do you disagree with?

7. Share three things you want to work on to lead more confidently as a woman in youth ministry.

# 4

# CAN I REALLY GET A (GOOD!) JOB IN YOUTH MINISTRY?

One of the reasons I accepted a youth ministry position at a large Southern California church several years ago was because they had a Starbucks on campus. Just kidding. Truthfully, it was because I'd have the privilege of overseeing the female youth ministry interns and volunteers on staff. After doing youth ministry for more than a decade—almost two—while raising a family, I now make it a point to encourage and equip other women in youth ministry.

I get a lot of questions from women of all ages who are interested in doing youth ministry. One of the questions or unspoken fears of not only the girls who are interested in pursuing youth work, but also the parents who might be helping to pay their college tuition is "Will they get a job?" In other words, is it a legit career choice for a GIRL to be a youth pastor, youth worker, coordinator, director, or other similar job title? Well, yes…and no! Let me explain.

Let's be honest, having a lucrative career in youth ministry—one that can financially sustain a family or pay all of your bills—is tough for anyone to achieve. Guy or girl. If you are exceptional, and by that I mean talented, gifted, called, and in the right place at the right time, you can get a decent and maybe even a well-paying youth ministry job. But don't underestimate the power of being bivocational. Getting a "real job," so to speak, on Monday through Friday so you can be free to do ministry when, where, and how you want is a beautiful gift! Bob Goff, speaker and author of *Love Does*, calls it "fundraising" for ministry as he heads to work as a lawyer. He uses his income to serve the kingdom of God and fund the ministry he does when he isn't working.

Liz, a youth worker I met at an area youth worker network lunch, is a full-time nurse. She works long shifts three days a week, and then she leads the youth ministry at her church for a small hourly salary when she isn't doing her "real job." Needless to say, she is a pretty busy woman in youth ministry. And she isn't doing it for the money. Not even close! In an article titled "The End of Paid Youth Ministry?" published in the May/June 2014 issue of *Group Magazine*, the data suggest that an increasing percentage of youth workers don't work full-time youth ministry jobs. For 36 percent, it's their second job and not their primary source of income. "The percentage of youth pastors working a second job is now more than double what it was in any survey since 2005!"[11] So, while you *can* get a full-time youth ministry position, the data suggest a high percentage of youth workers today are part time, bivocational, or volunteer.

Some of the most effective and faithful youth leaders I know are volunteers. I think of Bart and Connie, grandparents who open their home every Wednesday night and lead a small group for eleventh and twelfth graders in the South Bay area of San Diego. They've been ministering to teenagers at their church consistently and faithfully—and for longer than the long line of paid youth workers who've come and gone during that time.

I also think of Barbara who works for AT&T, and Sonia who works as a school nurse. None of these people have gone to seminary. They're not on the payroll at their church. Yet all of them are very much youth workers who've put in more time, sweat, tears, and consistent care for these teenagers than the revolving door of paid youth pastors. But what if you're certain that you're being called to youth ministry and you really want to make it your profession? What if, like myself, it's your dream to be in full-time vocational youth ministry?

First of all, it's important to have others who can affirm this call. Do your mentors, youth leaders, and friends see this as a good fit? Do they see God's calling in your life? Have you done volunteer youth ministry? Do you get asked or begged to teach, lead, or run the youth ministry? If you're volunteering in a youth group now, be self-reflective and aware of how that's really going. Are you asked to do more and more? Sometimes a youth pastor might be too afraid of hurting your feelings to be honest and tell you that youth ministry probably shouldn't be your career. Don't be afraid to examine your skill set and make sure you do have a clear and undeniable call to vocational youth ministry.

If you've been doing youth ministry (paid or volunteer) for a while, are you good at it? This is the all-important question to ask and prayerfully discern *before* you jump into a pile of student loan debt or change your major. Being relational and good with teenagers doesn't necessarily mean that youth ministry should be your career. Some of the best youth workers are volunteers who serve primarily in their sweet spot (doing only what they're good at) and don't collect a paycheck from a church or parachurch organization. Volunteers don't have to be good on stage, and they aren't required to deliver an awesome sermon or know how to communicate effectively with parents either. Volunteers don't necessarily have to be as organized as they would if youth work were their vocation.

I believe everyone is called into youth ministry on some level, just in terms of stewarding the now and the not yet of the next generation. But let's be honest: Not everyone should make a career of it. You may have grown up *loving* youth group; however, that doesn't mean you will *love* (or be any good at) vocational youth ministry. I've seen my share of socially awkward youth ministry Bible majors who clearly chose youth ministry because they loved their own youth group experience as teens. Youth group was their happy place, and it became their identity and place of belonging. Don't make youth ministry *your* thing. It has to be a God thing. A calling God is leading you into.

I don't think everyone who's interested in youth ministry should get an undergraduate degree in Bible or youth ministry, but many should seriously think about it. Following God's crystal clear call into vocational ministry can be scary. Really scary. I know what you may be thinking: *What the heck am I going to do with an undergraduate youth ministry degree if I change my mind?* But let's say you know God is leading you into ministry, and others have affirmed your calling. Then *why not* seriously consider getting a Bible or youth ministry degree? Don't be afraid to take off those arm floaties—or the security of that "real degree" your parents want you to get—and jump into the deep end of the pool. How many people do you know who have undergraduate degrees they don't use? Maybe a history major manages your local Home Depot. Or perhaps an engineering major is now the high school art teacher.

Pursuing an undergraduate degree while doing a really great youth internship played a huge role in landing my first full-time gig. I've seen many women get paid youth ministry jobs that might have otherwise gone to a guy because they had a degree and an internship experience to make them the more valuable candidate. Any church that takes you seriously as a professional (and pays you enough of an income to sort of live on) will want you to have a degree or be working toward getting one. My BA in Biblical Studies (with that ever-so-fun youth ministry emphasis) opened doors for me. Continuing on in seminary made me an even more valuable asset to keep around. As a youth pastor, I lean on my seminary degree from Azusa Pacific University quite a lot.

But what if you really are not called to youth ministry? How do you avoid continuing down the vocational youth ministry road without being one of those people who's oblivious that it's a bad fit for you? Before you change your entire life, or change your major, both men and women who are thinking about a career in youth ministry need to do this one thing (and it's a hard thing): Give someone permission to tell you the truth. Find someone you respect in vocational youth ministry and give that person permission to tell you what he or she *really* thinks. Some people are better suited as volunteers or behind-the-scenes ministry helpers than they are professional paid clergy.

## TO GET A DEGREE OR NOT TO GET A DEGREE?

As a professor at Indiana Wesleyan University, I have many students who come to me saying things like, "Well, I really want to be a youth pastor, but my parents said to major in business and then use my business degree to do youth ministry when I graduate." This is fine in theory, but what it means is that this business major is now competing against 80 other graduates who have an actual degree in youth ministry. And because of the integrative nature of our program, the youth ministry majors they are competing against often have pretty impressive résumés after internship requirements, etc. This is especially true for our female students!

So many young women come to me at the end of their junior year saying, "I wanted to major in youth ministry, but I thought I'd better major in elementary education so I'd have something to fall back on." Again, these women are up against youth ministry majors, and the large majority of them end up doing their backup plan instead of going for what God called them to do in the first place. In my context, women need a youth ministry degree even more than the men do—it can give them such a boost in confidence, competence, and calling.

— *Amanda Drury*

Every youth pastor I know has had a "wannabe" youth pastor on their ministry team at some point. Typically this person is a Bible major who is *not* good with adolescents, but is socially awkward, a boring teacher, emotionally immature, and really bad at dealing with the parents. Yet, most paid youth pastors will never tell a wannabe that they don't think he or she should become a youth pastor. So if you're wondering about your call to vocational ministry, *please* give your pastors and mentors a way to graciously and honestly advise you. There are men and women whom I wish someone had been kind enough to sit down with them before they spent thousands of dollars on a degree they will likely never use.

Sometimes difficult conversations need to happen and dreams need to die so that better ones can begin to grow. Make sure you're not one of those aspiring youth pastors being kept in the dark because a youth ministry professor or mentor isn't being honest with you. Ask the tough questions.

You know you've got "it" when everyone affirms your call and skills for vocational youth ministry. Back in the late '90s when I was young and just getting started, I traveled to Bakersfield, California, to teach a "speaking to teenagers" workshop for Youth for Christ. My youth ministry professor and mentor had recommended me to fill in for him. He wasn't able to do the gig, and I'd just finished his class on "Dynamic Communication."

The youth pastors who sat in my YFC workshop did two things:

**1. They said I shouldn't have told them I was in college.**
"We never would have guessed you were only a college sophomore. We all assumed you were a graduate. You carry yourself so well. Next time, don't tell people how old you are." Tip for young leaders: Let them assume you're older than you are.

**2. They gave me their business cards.** "Here is my card. I'd love to hire you once you graduate."

This event solidified in my mind that I was called to ministry. They affirmed my gifts, and I discovered I was good at teaching and equipping people. When men and women in ministry trust you to fill in for them, beg to hire you, or are surprised because you act older than you are, chances are good that you're called into vocational ministry. Or at least you don't suck at it.

So now what? How do women get legitimate jobs in youth ministry? Let me tell you how. First, you need to **pray**. Pray a lot.

Second, you need to **intern** somewhere that will open doors for you. So many guys and girls I know get great youth ministry positions because they put in time as a youth intern in a large church or reputable parachurch ministry. When girls or guys complete an internship at a large church, they're more likely to get jobs than those who don't. Fair or not, because of the size and notoriety of larger churches, their interns often get a better shot at the better (paid) youth ministry jobs as well.

I landed my first full-time youth ministry position because of an internship in a high-profile church. It was a great addition to my résumé. As a female in youth ministry, it's important to look for the right internship that will help get you where you want to go. And if you have a "large church" internship experience, chances are good you'll beat out guys and girls who did not. It really opened doors for me in the beginning. It's also opened doors for the young women who've interned for me in the present as well. Be strategic about where you intern. It can make a big difference in your future ministry options.

The third thing you must do is **network**. Find a local youth ministry network and be active in it. Don't limit yourself to only denominational or parachurch gatherings. It's a great way to build relationships and find potential employers. I know I've gotten youth ministry positions in the past largely due to being well connected with friends in the youth worker community. It's also a great way to let others know you're looking for an internship, a job, or a part-time gig. You can find out about potential openings and get great advice on how to interview and what to look for in a church from other youth workers in your local network.

You should have an idea about the kind of career you want to have in youth ministry. Once you do, meet other women who do what you want to do and pick their brains. Get to know them. See how they balance life as a female in youth ministry. Seek out others who can coach and mentor you in your calling.

Mariah, a recent intern in our youth department, is really good about networking and rubbing shoulders with those who can mentor her. From the moment I met her, I knew she had "it." She is sociable and creative, she loves Jesus, she's great in front of a group, she has amazing people skills, and she's clearly a good fit for youth ministry. She was barely 18 when she started her three-year internship with us. And after she completed it, she easily landed a paid youth ministry job. In fact, more than one church was interested in hiring her for their youth ministry staff. Mariah was leading an entire ministry by the age of 20.

Mariah did what I encourage all women pursuing youth ministry to do. She put in the time. She completed her internship at a large church where her gifts and calling shined bright. She squeezed room into her schedule—amidst the piles of homework and a packed ministry calendar—to attend youth ministry network meetings. She put her face and her name out there. When it came time to find a job, she had her pick of offers. After Mariah got hired, I showed my (then) seven-year-old daughter a picture of "Pastor Mariah" on

Facebook because I want my daughter to grow up knowing she can be female and get a *real* job in youth ministry.

Like in any other career field…a youth ministry job is just that. A job. And a position usually won't land in your lap. You have to work hard, be the best in your field, and compete for it just like in any other profession. Even though it's ministry, it's still very much a business. You're likely competing with a large stack of résumés for the same position. And this is especially true if it's a full-time position offering competitive pay. Keep your eyes and ears open.

A Facebook friend who teaches youth ministry classes at a seminary in Indiana posted that four youth ministry positions had been sent her way from churches looking for candidates. An hour before that, an interim youth pastor sitting next to me at a youth ministry network lunch told me her church had received a stack of 40 résumés for their youth pastor position. A week later, a pastor friend in Washington posted a job opening on her Facebook page. So you must network, which includes extending your own "social network" on Facebook with new and old ministry friends, because it's a great way to find ministry job openings. If I were looking for a new gig right now, I'd have several leads to pursue.

Also, just like in any other career, you have to go where the jobs are. If you want to stay within a certain geographic location or stay within a particular denomination, you will have fewer job options. And unfortunately for women who apply for youth ministry positions in conservative evangelical churches, the odds are not in your favor simply because of your gender.

When I think back on my undergraduate Bible college days, I can remember men walking out of chapel just because a female was speaking on that particular day. I also remember sitting in the auditorium of one of my previous, longtime church homes—a big Southern Baptist church—watching this tall,

# IT'S OUR TURN TO EMPOWER YOUNG WOMEN

I didn't know I could pastor teenagers. When I received the call to ministry, I was 17 years old and in a conservative denomination having never met a female youth minister. Being the only female in what's traditionally been a men's career was certainly a daring challenge to accept, but it didn't stop me from pursuing what I believed to be God's mission for my life. After I began blogging about my story—partly as a way to search for women who could prove it *is* possible to be a female youth pastor—I realized I wasn't alone. Still, it wasn't until I was two years into my first youth director role that I met a real-life female serving in full-time ministry. And it wasn't until a year ago that I heard a woman preach.

I've been blessed to be able to transition into a denomination in which I'm no longer a minority. As I share my story with others, they can hardly believe someone would tell me I can't do ministry. In fact, I'd almost forgotten about it myself until I had the privilege of teaching at a friend's church. Afterward, multiple girls came up to me and told me how meaningful it was for them to hear from a female youth minister. It had been *their* first time. I now have young women reaching out to me through my blog, telling me about the challenges they're facing as they pursue a career in ministry.

Our greatest challenges in life usually circle back to become our greatest points of ministry, and now I'm on the hunt to tell young women they can be anything they want to be—even and *especially* a youth pastor.

— *Heather Lea Campbell*

blond, beautiful, and skilled female musician perform. She'd appear as a musical guest a few times a year. Everyone *loved* her. And in between songs she'd talk...or share...or, in my mind, "preach." I'd sit there feeling a little bit ticked because (1) I have *zero* musical skills, and (2) I knew that if I ever wanted to "share" or "teach" or "preach" in my church, I'd have to take vocal lessons, be invited as a guest musician, and then slip bits of my sermon in between the songs. It was depressing. I can't sing. I'm not tall, blond, or musical. So there was no hope. I felt like my gifts had serious limitations.

This gender bias isn't unique to youth ministry. Take a look at the #GirlsCan: Women Empowerment COVERGIRL ad on YouTube. Go on. Get on YouTube[12] and look it up. You'll see a lineup of female celebrities sharing the things they've been told they can't do. Women such as Queen Latifah, Katy Perry, Ellen DeGeneres, P!nk, Janelle Monáe, Becky G, and ice hockey star Natalie Wiebe all share how #GirlsCan.

Jobs might seem scarce for women in youth ministry, but if you aren't limited by geography or denomination, many more options become available with more opportunities to use all of your gifts. I recommend you read books like *Lean In* by Sheryl Sandberg or *Bossy Pants* by Tina Fey to see how the job market can be tough for women in any industry and how gender discrimination, gender bias, and double standards are everywhere. These challenges are not unique to the Church. Yet, look at Sheryl and Tina. They are great at what they do, and they're successful because of their dedication to be the best in their fields. They work hard and lead well.

If you're great at what you do, you can have the youth ministry career you've always wanted. But it's not going to be easy. There are fewer youth ministry positions than there used to be, so it's a very competitive market. I'm very thankful I've never been without a youth ministry job. Networking, developing myself professionally, being willing to move, and not limiting myself to a particular denomination has contributed to landing the positions I've wanted. And I also remind myself that #GirlsCan.

# QUESTIONS FOR REFLECTION

1. What is your current role/position or involvement in youth ministry?

2. If you're pursuing youth ministry as a career, have you done the hard work and given permission to your closest friends, professors, and mentors to be honest with you regarding whether or not they affirm your call to vocational youth ministry?

3. What is your college or educational background? What dreams do you have for what's next?

4. What are the benefits of being a bivocational youth worker or a volunteer in youth ministry instead of being paid staff?

5. If you're in paid vocational youth ministry, what is the job market like for women in youth ministry in your area or denomination?

6. What tips do you have for finding a "good job" in youth ministry?

7. What are you really good at? Do you have the opportunity to use your gifts, your ideas, and your talents in the place where you serve or work? Why or why not?

8. What's your response to COVERGIRL's #GirlsCan ad?

9. What did you agree with in this chapter? What challenged you? What did you disagree with?

# 5

# SELFISHLY NETWORK

As a full-time youth worker, one thing I've always been committed to and am a huge advocate of is networking. Even when I have little time to spare (and who doesn't?), I set aside time each month to be a part of my local youth ministry network. A youth worker network is a group of youth pastors within a community who meet once a month (food is usually involved) to talk about ministry and grow together professionally and spiritually. The goal is to support each other's call to youth ministry.

While working in San Diego, I made it a point to be active in my local youth ministry network because it was a huge plus to my ministry, my soul, my sanity, and my longevity in ministry. Not every network meeting was a slam dunk or ended up being the best use of my time that day. But a long-term commitment to a local youth ministry network is worth it. Really, it is.

A year ago my family moved to Michigan. So now that I'm the "new girl" in town and doing youth ministry in Grand Rapids, *networking is even more vital*! A critical element to successfully beginning youth ministry in a new place is learning about your new community. So, yup, I've tracked down my local network and jumped right in. I was a little

## IT'S NOT WHAT YOU KNOW...

Have a network of people to encourage and pray for you. This
could be a family friend who's encouraged your ministry for a
long time, a colleague from across town, and someone who's
been a mentor to you. These people can be the ones you turn to
when you need insight, prayer, or a cheerleader to remind you of
how God has gifted you.

— *Carmen Garrigan*

worried I'd be the only female. (I wasn't.) And I briefly
wondered if they'd question my theology since I was coming
from Southern California and now working at a more
progressive church than what's typical for the area. (They
didn't.)

I chose to get involved in my local network—both in Grand
Rapids and in San Diego—*not* because it helps me reach more
students (even though it often does). I don't network because
we are "better together" (even though we are), nor because I
want to partner with other youth workers to add more shared
events to my calendar. In fact, I often *refuse* to leave a network
meeting with more things added to my calendar! "No, I *will not*
help with any See You at the Pole Rallies (so 1998), host any
youth crusades, or participate in anymore area-wide events..."
That's not my thing. And that's not why I network with other
youth workers. I don't need more to do. (But you'll get no
judgment from me if that's your kinda thing.)

I network for completely selfish reasons. Like free food,
laughs, friends, and the chance to share about the stupid things
my boss said or stories of ridiculousness that only other youth
workers can appreciate. Every youth worker needs to spend
time with other youth workers who understand your unique
calling (and can't fire you). We need people in our lives that we
can be *real* with...sharing our fractured selves without fear of

repercussion. I suspect that if you want to enjoy your calling as a youth worker, and if you're able to carve out two hours a month for your own sanity, then you should also join a youth ministry network. Here's why:

*1. You'll meet people who do what you do.* Sometimes (maybe even oftentimes) other youth workers have great ideas that make your ministry better. You can also contribute to the youth ministry tribe via your local network by sharing your best ideas, resources, and experiences. The youth workers in your town, who serve in your community, "get" your unique context. They understand your challenges and the culture of where you lead. Blogs and professional conferences can't do this as effectively. And as a relative newcomer to West Michigan, this has been helpful for me because the Midwestern culture is *a lot different* than the one in San Diego. Plus, just by showing up, I discovered where to find good Chinese food. There's a wealth of knowledge to be found all in one room.

*2. You'll meet other women in youth ministry.* A WIN!! You need to show up so the men can see there are a lot of female youth workers in town. And also because other women in youth ministry *from your community* will be there. Meet each other. Be purposeful. Don't be shy. Make plans to take each woman to lunch or coffee at some point. This is *so* encouraging and fun and helpful and *totally worth it.* These women know your challenges, your desire to lead well, and all that you have to juggle as a female in a male-dominated profession. And since they don't go to *your* church, you can talk smack if *ya* want and no one will judge you or report you to the senior pastor.

*3. You'll meet parachurch youth workers.* The Young Life peeps, the Campus Life directors, and the FCA staff often attend these network meetings. They are well connected and know *a lot* about the youth culture in *your* community (which can be very different than the culture among your youth group students). They know a lot about local schools. This is so stinking valuable. They know the teachers, principals, coaches, community resources, and important people in town. Parachurch youth workers have connections with local businesses and organizations who are supportive of youth ministry. These are youth workers you need to know and learn from—especially if you're a new youth worker or new in town. Ask one of them to give you a tour of the city and teach you more about the community you're serving. Don't miss these people! You can learn so freakin' much from them. I promise!

**4. You might work with or work for one of them one day.** Maybe you're looking for a youth ministry job. Maybe you recently graduated from college and want an internship. Maybe you're getting fired next month and you don't know it yet. (That would suck.) Or maybe you want to quit your youth ministry job and need to talk to someone (who doesn't go to your church) about what you're thinking. Booya! The local youth worker network is perfect for this! You might have a best friend or spouse to talk through stuff with; but unless they're also youth workers, chances are good they don't "get it" like these people do.

Your local youth ministry network is where someone will tell you about a youth ministry opening that hasn't gone public yet. They know who is working where, who is moving, who is quitting, who might be getting fired, who is looking for a paid intern, and so on. *You want to know these people* because you never know when you'll be so glad you do. They might even be the peeps who bring you a lasagna after an overnighter gone bad, buy you coffee because you seem discouraged, or hire you as a speaker for their next summer camp. Be selfish and get to know these people.

**5. You won't look like a snob.** It's amazing to me how many "big church" youth workers resist going to local youth worker network meetings. Even in San Diego, the youth workers from the bigger churches often got a bad rap because the only time they came to a meeting was when they were hosting some ultra huge event they wanted to invite the other youth groups to attend. There was no sense of community or identification with the rest of the tribe beyond a "stop-n-drop," where they merely stopped by to drop off a stack of their flyers for the big gig. Even in Grand Rapids and other networks I've consulted with or gone to visit, it's rare to have the megachurch youth workers show up. Now, they might not be showing up for perfectly valid reasons, like they don't know you have a network, or the network meeting is always during their mandatory all-church staff meeting. But even so, with every absence a negative "us versus them" vibe gets perpetuated (intentionally or not).

When I served as a youth pastor at a large church, I know that whenever I made an effort to show up at a network meeting, it always reflected positively upon my church. It helped the other area youth pastors see my church as a part of their community, not some strange unknown competition down the street.

When youth workers from the megachurch or multisite church show up, it sends a powerful message of "we are all in this together." The job titles and attendance numbers get left at the door, and the youth workers—regardless of church size—come together as one. When youth workers from the little church down the street and that large church across town that causes all the traffic problems on Sunday mornings choose to hang out together, people notice. Students notice. And our perspective changes. Now instead of feeling as though I lost a student from my youth group to "that other church," I know my student is being looked after and shepherded by friends and youth pastors I know and trust.

We model family when we come together. We provide better care and pastoring when we know each other. We can say to a student, "Oh, you're going to Pastor Christina's youth group on Friday nights? That's awesome! She's one of my friends and you will love her!" *instead of* "Why don't you come to youth group anymore?" Which response better reflects the body of Christ?

**6. You'll meet youth workers from outside your own denominational affiliations and size.** Branch out beyond your own people. Diversity makes us better. Get to know youth workers from other denominations, theological perspectives, and cultures. Most of the people in my local network are from really small churches. It's been a decade since I worked at a small church. They do tend to plan a lot of events together because if they didn't, there wouldn't be a critical mass to pull off a winter camp weekend or summer mission trip. I need to remember that. I need to support that. I need to remember that large or small, part of a mainline denomination or not, we are family. So, yes, I will lend you all my leftover art supplies for your interactive prayer room. Play nice and share.

My favorite quote that I've been thinking about lately is from *Divergent*:

*We are not the same. But we are, somehow, one.*[13]

When you stay with your own kind and network only within your own denomination (or gender), you fail to connect beyond yourself. When you hang out exclusively in a like-minded bubble, *you stay small.* If you want to lead well, grow, and love extravagantly, make it a point to mix it up with other youth workers who think, lead, and do things differently than you do. When you think your denomination or theological framework is the only right one, that's when you start to get it all wrong. Get a little uncomfortable and mingle with believers who are a little (or a lot) different than you.

**7. Sometimes you need to lose some to win big.** To be honest, not all of the area youth worker network meetings are a win. Sometimes they talk about stuff that has zero to do with my youth group or me. Sometimes it's a waste of time. A big waste of time. Yet, I go anyway. There might be four sucky waste-of-time meetings that go by, but because I am there regardless and putting in the relational investment into my local youth worker tribe, when it's a win—it's a BIG win. It can't be all about "what I get out of it"; it has to be more about what I put into it.

Faithful investment into local networks pays off because at some point we all get comfortable with each other. We all get to know and trust each other. Eventually we have that meeting where someone is honest and starts a real conversation. Then someone else gets more honest. The room gets vulnerable. The topics, the conversations, the sharing and praying get real and life-giving. The hour flies on by and you're on the verge of uncovering the stuff we're all dealing with but are too afraid to talk about. As the meeting wraps up, everyone feels closer and more connected, and we wish we could stay and talk all day because magic just happened. Because sometimes you need to go to four sucky meetings in order to get to the one you couldn't live without.

Network! You will all be the better for it. Youth ministry will be the better for it. You don't want to stay small. And, remember, a free lunch is *always* awesome.

So how does one find a local network? Ask around. Other youth workers in your area probably know if there is an official or unofficial youth ministry network in town. You can also take a peek at the National Network of Youth Ministries' listing of local networks.[14] If your network isn't listed there, be sure to add it so people can find you.

# QUESTIONS FOR REFLECTION

1. Are you involved in an area youth ministry network? Why or why not?

2. Why might meeting together with other youth workers from your community be helpful to your own youth ministry?

3. If you're part of a denomination, do you intentionally seek out ways to connect with other youth workers from outside of your denominational affiliation? Why or why not?

4. After reading through the list of reasons why you should "selfishly network" what stands out as your top one or two reasons to show up at your next network meeting?

5. Action Step: Find a youth worker (one you don't know yet) from a different church in town and take them out for coffee or lunch. Share ideas. Learn about each other's church and student ministry.

6. Action Step: If you're a parent or volunteer involved in youth ministry, take your own youth worker out to lunch and learn more about his or her vision, mission, and heart for the teens in your church.

# 6

# BREAKING BAD BOUNDARIES

B*reaking Bad* spoiler alert: At the end of the last episode of *Breaking Bad*, Walter White lies on the floor with a gunshot wound. And his former student and partner Jesse Pinkman drives away from the scene with tears in his eyes, kind of unsure about all that went down. What just happened?

Maybe you've felt like that before. Wondered how ministry could get so messy, hurtful, and damaging to your relationships and the people you care about. How can you protect your ministry relationships with other leaders and volunteers? Whether you are paid or volunteer, full time or part time, you can create an atmosphere for good communication and healthy working relationships within your ministry team. You just need to make sure you're sharing honestly with your colleagues in a timely way, instead of stuffing your feelings and getting resentful. And you also need to establish healthy boundaries around your work schedule to protect your family time. Doing these two things on a consistent basis will bring out the best in both you and those you work with.

# HEALTHY BOUNDARIES PROTECT YOUR DIGNITY

*The role and purpose of power in relationships
is to bestow dignity upon the other person.* #drbennett[15]

Most of us have probably had some kind of a fallout with
another person. After all, even the most patient and nicest
people among us have their limits. At one church where I
worked, I had a particularly tough fallout with a male youth
pastor. And I finally figured out how everything went south—
why my working relationship, which had started out so great,
ended so badly. Everything came into focus after I started
thinking about boundaries, complementary theology, and
communication. They all connect to each other, like a thread
woven through a sweater.

Churches with a hierarchical or complementarian view of
women in ministry (see chapter 1 for definitions of these terms)
tend to be the ones with multiple mandated [bad] boundaries
that often result in poor communication between men and
women. Boundaries designed to protect might actually be
hurting people and hindering job performance.

Sacred Friendship Gathering is an organization dedicated
to challenging the present understanding of boundaries
in friendships between men and women by encouraging
reconciliation and healthy engagement. It has this to say about
bold boundaries on the organization's website:

> *Bring up the subject of friendship between men and
> women and you'll find the subject of boundaries is close
> at hand....We have the best of intentions and we want
> to do the right thing. We build fences and draw lines
> in order to protect what we see as holy, sacred. This is
> good, admirable—but what if some of the boundaries
> we create are actually keeping us locked in?*[16]

It's time to break some bad. Too many boundaries between men and women working in ministry together actually *hurt* their job performance. Boundaries designed to keep things on the "up and up" might instead perpetuate a work atmosphere of brokenness. Broken communication. Broken relationships. A broken compensation scale. Broken people working in an unhealthy environment. Boundaries that keep us quietly "locked in" hinder healthy dialogue and growth.

Here's my fallout story: Looking back on that time now, I remember feeling weird about so many things and questioning if my youth ministry position was still a good fit for me. For example, I'd noticed that the male youth pastor drove his own vehicle on practically every ministry trip. Even when I was six months pregnant, the girl in charge "associate" (me) had to ride the bumpy school bus that reeked of corn nuts and stinky feet. And again as a nursing mom, I had to pump milk on a church bus while we were on our way to a camp. Meanwhile, the guy in charge drove his own car.

Each year before we'd load the buses for summer or winter camp, the youth pastor showed me off to the parents. He introduced me as a seasoned *youth pastor* with tons of experience. And he made sure they knew I was also a mom. (You can always trust a mom, right?) I was there to make the parents feel good about entrusting their kids to our ministry for a week at summer camp. I felt like I was the token full-time female on staff without the pastor title but with the pastoral housing allowance. I was there to dispense tampons, enforce the dress code, and comfort barfing kids with my mama mojo. So off to summer camp we go…most of us riding on school buses.

So now we're at summer camp, and the stomach flu is going around. Not fun. If you've ever held open a plastic bag for a vomiting middle schooler, you feel my pain. Nonetheless, the youth pastor still heads out for the annual fancy steak luncheon that the camp puts on for just the youth pastors. You know the kind. The "wow" lunch of the week that's designed to get them booking spots for winter camp and rebooking for summer camp next year. After the youth pastor left, one of the youth ministry volunteers looks over at me and asked, "Why don't you go to the youth pastor lunch? Aren't you considered the girl youth pastor?" I just shrugged it off, but inside I was wondering the exact same thing because in all my years of working on staff with him, he'd *never* let me go with him to the camp's youth pastor luncheon.

I grabbed a box of saltines and started the long walk back to the cabins full of puking middle school girls. Girls are sick. The sickness is spreading. It is bad. And it only gets worse. We're at a camp without good cell phone service, and we didn't bring walkie-talkies with us. So communication is a challenge. Especially when it starts getting late. Day turns to night and the camp is huge. It's no easy task to track someone down.

But now with the vomiting occurring so rampantly among the girls, a decision has to be made to send some of them home. Parents need to be called. Since I'm in charge of the girls, I make the decision and tell the camp nurse that I'm completely on board with the plan to call parents and send girls home. Together, the camp nurse and I arrange for a couple of girls to be picked up in the morning so they can vomit in the comfort of their own homes.

Fast-forward to the next morning at breakfast when the youth pastor finds out that girls from our youth group are going home without his prior knowledge. He is furious. I didn't have a chance to give him a heads-up (remember, bad cell service and no walkie-talkies). So when he finds out parents are already on their way, he yells at me. He also yells at the camp nurse for not clearing it with him first. He makes it clear that he is the youth pastor and *I am not*. Tears are shed. I am furious. I was hoping to hear, 'Thanks, Gina, for dealing with this," but instead I get yelled at during breakfast in front of everyone. Stripped of my dignity once again. How healthy are our ministries, really, if they model to our teenagers such negative treatment of women?

I'm wondering if this is what it means to work in a ministry with a "complementary view" of women in ministry. I thought I was the "girl youth pastor" operating within the confines of my acceptable role. But this didn't feel too complementary. It felt more like tyranny. As I continued to work through my own theology and its impact on my job satisfaction, I realized that even if he were to leave, retire, or get fired from this church, my gender would always keep me as number two on the youth ministry totem pole. For a while I was okay with that. There was plenty of youth ministry work to be done, so it didn't bother me as long as I could at least lead in the ministry areas that were listed in my job description. But in the aftermath of this camp catastrophe, I was discovering that even within my own role there were unspoken limitations being placed on me.

I longed to use all of my ministry gifts and lead the way my job description had implied. It wasn't happening. Anything that involved power, control, or decision making, the youth pastor held onto pretty tightly. After we returned home from camp, he started leaving me out of more and more of the ministry decision making. He even hired female youth staff without looping me in first, even though that was a part of my job. He began second-guessing my decisions and resisting any of my ideas, even when they were undeniably good ones. Like moving our student leader meetings to Wednesdays (before youth group) instead of Sundays. Our student leadership involvement skyrocketed after that. Everyone loved the change, but still he kept asking, "So should we move the meeting back to Sundays?" Thankfully, all of our staff answered loudly and in unison, "No!"

I don't mean to imply that I was an innocent bystander in all of this. Do you know what I did wrong? I wimped out and never said anything. All of these situations—the steak luncheon/night of vomit, being pregnant or pumping breast milk on a school bus, and the general misadventures of summer camp—could have been great lessons in communication for both of us and led to better ministry. I should have been more direct and told him how I was feeling. And if that didn't work, I could have reached out to our Christian education pastor or even our human resources director. But I didn't. I was too worried about being the "nice girl." When I did finally speak up, it was *way* too late.

Working in a patriarchal environment that never welcomed criticism or too many opinions had created an unhealthy silence, especially when it came to communication between men and women. The senior pastor at that church had made it very clear that he didn't pay critics when he could always get criticism for free. I understand what he meant, but comments like that from senior leadership only serve to perpetuate bad work practices. When people keep quiet and blindly support and regurgitate whatever comes down from on high, new and better ideas have a hard time rising to the surface. Bad work environments tend to stay that way. Why speak up and risk being fired? Rarely was anyone on staff authentic. No one was courageous enough to tell the truth.

I was challenged by what Sheryl Sandberg says about this:

> *Authentic communication is not always easy, but it is the basis for successful relationships at home and real effectiveness at work. Yet people constantly back away from honesty to protect themselves and others. This reticence causes and perpetuates all kinds of problems: uncomfortable issues that never get addressed, resentment that builds, unfit managers who get promoted rather than fired, and on and on. Often these situations*

*don't improve because no one tells anyone what is
really happening. We are so rarely brave enough to tell
the truth.*[17]

Bad communication and a lack of authenticity had definitely
created some toxic problems in our work environment. For
instance, you can imagine how shocked I was when this same
youth pastor who'd yelled at me at summer camp asked, "How
are you spending your time when I'm not around?" In my mind
I was working much harder than he was and reaching every
benchmark asked of me. So being accused of mismanaging my
time and abusing my schedule seemed so out of line. I wanted
to storm out like a five-year-old and say, "See ya later, sucka!"
But instead, I went on a walk and cried.

Note: If anyone ever asks you, "How do you spend your time?"
or asks you to document your time after you've already been
working there for a while, take it as a major warning sign. You
need to over-communicate your schedule and the use of your
time. Now I make it a point to mark everything on my calendar
and track what I'm working on each day.

Bad communication compounded by impeding boundaries
led to suspicion, distrust, and bitterness in our professional
relationship. Not a good recipe for working well together. In
the end we worked it out. Well, sort of. We parted ways and
I found a better ministry fit at another church. I've thought
a lot about this fallout over the years because *I'd never had
one before*. I am the ultimate people pleaser and overachiever
who goes out of my way to get along with everyone. So this
miscommunication that led to the end of a friendship and a
ministry partnership was really tough for me. I cried every day,
lost 10 pounds, and couldn't sleep. It was almost like a high
school breakup.

Looking back, the problem began as a mutual effort to be
"nice" by not sharing what we were really struggling with

as we worked together. I'm convinced our fallout was just a casualty of men and women working together in conservative, hyper boundary-enforced ministry where the fear of any suspicion or appearances of possible "moral failure" dominates the office chemistry and *kills* honest communication.

Bad boundaries created a cold and sterile work environment. It was a hug-free zone with everyone being held at arm's length. We were all waiting for ninjas or nuns to drop from the ceiling at any moment, with rulers in hand to enforce a safe distance between anyone and everyone. As a result, we experienced damaged work relationships. Boundaries and too many unspoken rules permeated the office mojo. They killed communication. I was never stifled by such boundaries when I worked at a Presbyterian church with an egalitarian view of women in leadership (where coed lunches are the norm not shunned). Theology really does shape everything…even office relationships.

Carefully drawn boundaries to keep things looking great and aboveboard on the outside began to *rot the relationships on the inside*. Keeping each other at arm's length is a wonderful recipe for respecting unofficial church-mandated boundaries, but it put a huge dent in creating an atmosphere for effective communication. Especially when it came to things like conflict. When men refuse to have lunch with, ride in cars with, or mentor women professionally, it's damaging to a respectful and thriving work atmosphere.

Depending on the culture and traditions of the church, an openness to communicate with the opposite sex in a ministry context can be uninviting and a huge challenge. In my experience, mainline Protestants (with egalitarian theology) are a lot better at it than conservative evangelicals. As I saw the unhealthy side of boundaries, dress codes, rigid rules about alcohol and tattoos, I began to question the theology and the bad boundaries I'd been accommodating without question.

Yes, I'd been honoring the established boundaries, but at what expense?

How many youth workers are intent on having affairs and looking to add sexual misconduct with their coworkers to their résumés? Not many. And for most of us, it's not even a palatable temptation. Yet all of us are made to suffer because of the few who ruined it for everybody. This happens more so in conservative churches, or churches that are still recovering after people crossed the line before we ever came along.

Just to be clear, I'm not talking about boundaries with teenagers. That's another issue altogether, and I will do whatever it takes to protect my students. What I'm talking about are the unnecessary boundaries between adults within a ministry context, which kills communication in the name of "appearances."

Do you suffer from major communication challenges because you're forced to walk on eggshells and care more about ministry appearances than authenticity? Unless you proactively go after it, great communication is not going to happen on its own. No matter where you work. Be intentional and make open communication a priority. Create safe places to share how you really feel before it turns something small into a gigantic mess of hurt feelings and mistrust. I respect boundaries, but not when they become more damaging than helpful to a ministry. So often the boundaries placed between men and women in ministry create more problems than the reasons for erecting those boundaries in the first place.

How can a man and woman work well together when the two of them can't even ride together in the same car or an elevator? Well, maybe the elevator is okay. But you can just forget about attending a ministry luncheon together or driving to a youth worker network meeting without a chaperone. So why on earth would we open up to each other in honest conversation?

A full-time male youth pastor and a full-time female youth associate working closely together while both are married to other people made us both hypersensitive to appearances and maintaining strong boundaries. It took five years to even get a side hug. We've been fist-bumping and high-fiving each other since college.

This youth pastor with whom I had so many communication problems would always take our administrative assistant with us as a chaperone for any car ride or lunch meeting. He could ride to meetings alone with men, but never with women. Even when we were driving to the same stinkin' place. My gender meant I had to drive myself. There were so many missed time-saving opportunities to talk ministry, plan events, and evaluate ministry programming. A lot of work could have been accomplished during those car rides and coed lunches.

I guess the bottom line for me was this: Keeping women separated from men in ministry made it feel wrong to be a female. It perpetuated a sense of shame and brokenness by keeping women at arm's length. Emily Maynard writes, "We cannot be a community of people who learn to love God and love others when it comes on the condition that one half of the community is a threat to the whole."[18]

Why should my gender keep me out of pastoral lunches and carpools to meetings? Even emails can get weird. Just the other day, I went to a youth pastor lunch. You know the kind: "Lunch is on us, but you have to listen to our spiel about some camp, youth event, or mission trip." This one was an all-you-can-eat gourmet pizza lunch. (Youth pastor meetings are dangerous to my dress size.) I was a tiny bit interested in the camp that the youth pastor sitting next to me was talking about. So he emailed me some more information the very next day, and he cc'ed his wife on the email. A dumb little email about summer camp.

I get why guys in ministry like to have rules and boundaries for their interactions with women, but really? Guys, would you have cc'ed your wife if that email had been sent to a male colleague? To him, he was being super husband dude. To me, I once again felt like just because I happen to wear lipstick, I'm some kind of threat. It didn't feel professional. It felt degrading.

Let's get real here. Viewing women (but not other men) as potential threats in order to avoid any "perception of wrongdoing" is dumb. It's shameful. It also assumes everyone is straight and not secretly struggling with their own sexual identity. Think about the controversies and misconduct of those you know locally or what you've heard on a national level. If someone is going to do something stupid, they're going to do it regardless of the existing boundaries, and it won't always be with people of the opposite sex.

It's far more helpful to create a working environment that fosters emotional and spiritual health. When staff walk and work together in wholeness, stupid doesn't happen. For communication to be healthy, for men and women to grow professionally and learn from one another, they need to be allowed to spend time together. Sheryl Sandberg shares, "Personal connections lead to assignments and promotions, so it needs to be okay for men and women to spend informal time together the same way men can."[19]

Break those bad boundaries. Be proactive in pursuing wholeness, not accentuating the brokenness in us all. Lead confidently from a place of mutual respect, not fear and shame. I'm not talking about hiding in dark corners alone, wining and dining your coworkers, or being alone with volunteers you barely know. I'm advocating for it to be okay to do simple things like drive to Starbucks for Frappy Hour (Starbucks speak for half-price ice blended Frappuccinos) and talk about your next youth retreat. Do you really need to drive in separate cars to do that?

When I talked to my Presbyterian pastor friend who thought nothing of coed lunches or carpooling with the opposite sex to a Presbytery meeting, I realized my situation was so not the norm. My boundaries were dumb.

But it took me awhile to realize I was stuck and damaged by unhealthy boundaries. To realize I was being silenced because of my gender. David Hayward wrote a post on his blog *NakedPastor* regarding a church very similar to the one in which I'd spent much of my life:

> *Silence is key to the success of the operation. Especially for women. I suggest there can only be two explanations for how this is happening:*
>
> *1. The women are not self-aware enough to realize they are being oppressed; or*
> *2. They do realize it but...[they also] realize it's easier to be quiet and capitulate rather than fight for their rights.*
>
> *Like I already said, this only works if the people keep quiet. So I'm sending out a signal to all of you under this kind of regime: it's time to start talking.*
>
> *I promise if you do it will topple soon.*[20]

I really wanted to start talking. I wasn't the youth pastor because I wasn't male. I was a powerless youth ministry associate who was stuck enforcing dress code, driving alone to meetings, having to give an accounting for my time, and doing whatever I was told. I wasn't allowed to question or move our ministry forward. Then I got unstuck. I broke some bad. I figured out my boundaries. What I was okay with and what I would no longer tolerate. I wanted my dignity back.

*If we want to cultivate more courage, joy, and love in our lives, we have to understand how and why shame keeps us afraid and small.*[21]
— *Brené Brown*

Wanna break bad boundaries? Take someone of the opposite gender out to lunch. Jesus didn't keep women at arm's length. He didn't ice them out of his personal space. Remember the lady wiping Jesus' feet with her hair? Or how about the woman who touched his robe while she was having a never-ending period? After she touched Jesus, she was no longer isolated from the community because of her feminine bleeding. Twelve years a slave and now she was set free. No administrative assistant or chaperone could block her access or proximity to Jesus. That notion would totally freak out a bunch of the men I used to work with.

A Sacred Friendship Gathering says this:

> *In the Gospels we see Jesus expanding personal, social, and spiritual boundaries to draw near to women in unprecedented ways and include them as his friends in the kingdom of God. His boundaries were fundamentally inclusive, not exclusive, and worked directly against the old order of lust, sexism, suspicion, distance, violence, and oppression between men and women.*[22]

I'm happy to say that today I'm enjoying healthier boundaries. Breaking bad boundaries helped me to love my calling as a woman in youth ministry again. I recently had lunch with one of our program staff guys. He took me to lunch because he knows how important it is for me to communicate well with the men I work with. He knows all about the weirdness I came from, and he wanted to show me "it's not like that here." Plus, I needed lunch, he needed lunch, and we had some ministry work we needed to talk about. It's a huge timesaver for me to be able to accomplish ministry tasks while doing the normal things of life…like eating or driving somewhere. So go lunch it up already. Break bad over a burger.

## HEALTHY BOUNDARIES PROTECT YOUR TIME

Breaking bad boundaries is about more than just protecting your relationships with coworkers; it also means protecting your time. Youth workers can have a difficult time establishing boundaries to protect their "me time" or homework time or family time. By tracking your time, you'll find proof that there is no such thing as "part-time ministry" and proof that you're working more than almost humanly possible.

Everyone laughs at the idea of part-time ministry. You've heard it said over and over again: There is no such thing as part-time ministry, only part-time pay. It's so true, especially when you're wired for ministry. It's something we do. Whether we're on the clock or not. Dan Crouch, a youth worker in the Church of England, shares in an interview posted on *ChurchLeaders. com*:

### BEGINNINGS AND ENDINGS

One tip I learned from my husband is to have an end time for meetings. I really enjoy working collaboratively in meetings, but in the ministry world I've discovered we have a bad habit for being ambiguous about when we'll be done. When you plan a meeting, set an end time in addition to a start time. And when you agree to a meeting, ask for an end time. This helps you organize your schedule and keeps everyone on track when you meet, so you can get back home to hang out with your spouse.

—*Carmen Garrigan*

*I worked 37 hours on paper, but in reality it was more like 50. It's probably not healthy, but that's the reality of being in youth ministry. A minister is never working 37 hours a week; it's not a 9-5 job. The issues young people have don't wait until a more convenient time. In September the church had to reduce my hours to 29, but I still work about 40.*[23]

I've found that keeping a log of how I spend my time is really helpful. First, I can see if I'm too heavy on the admin/office hours and too light on the ministering *with people* hours. It's easy to hide behind a computer and not spend time with teenagers and staff outside of program time. Tracking my time helps me stay in check. The question to ask is, "Am I spending my time in the areas that best help me meet my ministry goals?" A good reminder to post on my mirror: I WANT TO BE A MINISTER NOT AN ADMINISTRATOR.

Second, tracking your time or logging your hours is a fantastic tool for making sure you workaholics are honoring your days off. Do you protect your calendar enough to enjoy your friends and family? When I see my work hours are way exceeding what I actually get paid to do, I know I need to slow down and spend more time on the home front. Tracking your time is a great tool for raising awareness of all the extra time you work without even realizing it.

How often are you up late checking and replying to church emails? What about when you're hanging with zombies and watching *The Walking Dead* on TV, only to find yourself updating your youth group webpage during the episode? Or maybe you're designing a youth group flyer right before you go to bed? Every little minute adds up, and I bet you'd be shocked to see how many hours a week you *really* work in ministry.

If you work from home, then tracking your time is a must to protect your family and work time. When I start my "timer" and I'm on the work clock, I'm less likely to be sidetracked by laundry, dishes, or Facebook. When I'm on the clock, I'm on the clock. The next time someone rolls their eyes when you pack up your laptop to go "work from home," you can prove

# NO, I DON'T WORK 50 HOURS A WEEK...OR DO I?

When I started youth ministry during college, the idea of setting boundaries wasn't on my youth ministry checklist. My thoughts were, *I'm jumping right in. I'm going to form great relationships ASAP. I'm going to learn everything about these students as fast as I can. I'm going to be available to them at all hours. I'm going to plan a ton of events. It's going to be awesome!* Now, after spending more than 10 years in youth ministry, my thoughts have radically changed. I've learned that setting boundaries in all areas is vital to the survival of any youth worker.

Some questions I had to ask myself include: *What do my boundaries look like for events? How many will I do? How many weekends will I work? When will I turn off my phone? When is it okay to leave an email unanswered? When is it okay not to return a text? Can I even say no to things?*

Sometimes figuring out the answers to these questions can seem unimportant, but knowing my boundaries, setting them, and making them known has been a valuable lesson that I learned later in my career. And once these boundaries were made known, I was able to rest and take better care of my soul. Students knew I'd probably be sleeping by 10 p.m. Parents knew we planned one special event each month. The church staff knew Thursday was my day off. With proper boundaries in place, this opened up an important and mutual understanding of areas where I was blessed to say yes and no.

Boundaries will look different to each youth worker—and they should. My encouragement would be to prayerfully consider what a healthy work week looks like to you and decide what boundaries need to be set up in order to fulfill the very important goal of having a healthy and rested soul.

— *Angie Williamson*

that you really do work from home by keeping track of your time. Record not just how many hours you logged from home, but what exactly you worked on too. It's a beautiful way to work from home guilt-free and kick some butt with all that you get done!

How do you track working hours without it being more trouble than it's worth? I've found a web app called Cashboard that seems to be the best solution for me to see how I spend my work hours.[24] (Bonus: Small churches can use Cashboard to track camp deposits and registration fees too.) Now if someone asks me, "What do you do all day?" I can place a handy time report in their hands and watch them flinch a bit.

A less costly (but also less dazzling) way to do this is to simply log everything into Google Calendar or iCalendar. Everything you do—all of the appointments, sermon prep time, shopping for youth group snacks, etc.—should be posted on your calendar. Then be sure to share your calendar with your supervisor, administrative assistant, and colleagues. They won't have to wonder where you've been, and they can easily see why you might need to say no to that extra committee meeting or project because you've logged way too many hours already.

# QUESTIONS FOR REFLECTION

1. How and when can boundaries between male and female colleagues be helpful?

2. How might boundaries hinder communication between men and women who work in ministry together?

3. What official or unspoken rules and boundaries exist between the male and female staff in your ministry (if any)?

4. Look up Mark 5:24-34, Luke 7:36-50, and John 4:1-26. How did Jesus interact with women? What can we learn from these passages?

5. How do you handle conflict and miscommunication with male coworkers?

6. How might egalitarian or complementarian theology influence and shape ministry work environments between men and women?

7. What about time boundaries? Do you track your hours? Why or why not?

8. Action Step: Track all of your time for a week and see what you learn. Don't pick a week when you're at camp. Pick a typical ministry week and log your hours.

9. Are you good at protecting your family or personal time? Or do you allow ministry to take over?

# 7

# ADVICE FOR WORKING WELL WITH MEN IN YOUTH MINISTRY

How do men and women work well in ministry together? For me, I've had many great experiences working with guys in youth ministry, and only a few bad ones. It can be hard not to dwell on the times when things got weird and hurtful between male and female colleagues, but overall the two sexes do work pretty well together in ministry.

For men and women to work closely and still maintain open communication and happy office dynamics, several things need to happen.

**First, get to know each other's personality and leadership styles**. This will be an incredibly helpful tool for discovering each other's motivations, strengths, and weaknesses. Figure out who is an introvert or extrovert. If you don't already have a favorite leadership inventory tool or behavior analysis such as the Myers-Briggs personality inventory, find one.[25] My new favorite is the Enneagram.[26]

**Second, figure out your work rhythms, creative times, and don't-interrupt-me times.** My male co-pastor and I figured out that neither one of us is conversational in the morning. Kyle oversees the younger students in our ministry, and I oversee the older ones. We work closely together on all things "middle school." We say hello and that's about it until we've each had a couple cups of coffee and it's past 10 a.m. We tend to work quietly and independently until later in the morning. And to stop me from constantly interrupting whatever he's working on with my overzealousness for ideation, we have a scheduled meeting once a week during which we talk through programming and touch base with each other. So I try to save all of my ideas and would-be interruptions for this time.

**Third, get to know each other's gifts, strengths, and areas of interest.** I am an "idea" person and storyteller. Kyle is a deep thinker and super smart. While I'm testing the best angle for throwing toilet paper through toilet seats suspended from the youth room ceiling, Kyle will be sitting at his desk with stacks of commentaries lying open as he works on curriculum content. I suck at doing anything on the spot, like being funny and energetic on stage without some practice. Kyle can create momentum on a moment's notice. I like giving middle schoolers candy. Kyle would rather hand out yogurt and apple slices. Because we know each other's gifts, interests, strengths, and weaknesses, we're able to leverage that knowledge to be the best ministry team we can be. We don't compete with each other; we work together and bring "balance to the force."

**Fourth, share your calendar with each other and over-communicate.** Don't give your colleagues any reason to

## GET TO THE HEART OF THE MATTER

While men and women are certainly wired differently, there are heart issues that we all share. A man might express envy, stress, fear, and doubt differently than a woman does, but ultimately we're all in need of the same grace—from each other and from God.

— *Carmen Garrigan*

wonder what you're up to. My coworkers can see everything on my calendar. If I leave the office early because I need to take my nine-year-old to Girl Scouts, I make sure to say just that. If I'm working off site at a coffee shop for an hour or two, it's on my calendar. There are no "Gee, where have you been all day?" wonderings. If I'm doing lesson prep or writing parent emails, I make a note of it on my calendar. If something comes up like a sick kid or a death in the family—cover for each other. If you need help, communicate that and work hard to help each other be successful. Having someone who "has your back" at work is a beautiful thing!

**Fifth, remind male pastors and volunteers to introduce female staff right away.** When you show up at an event, camp, or conference with one of the guys you do youth ministry with, don't give anyone time to assume you're his wife, daughter, girlfriend, or administrative assistant (unless you are). Take the initiative to confidently introduce yourself right away and share what you do. Something like, "Hey, I'm Sue and I lead the girls' small groups." Or "I'm Gina, the middle school pastor, and this is Kyle, the Fifty6 pastor."

**Sixth, praise in public...confront in private...and *never do it over email or text*.** Brag about each other to your ministry supervisors and coworkers. Compliment a job well done. If something is going on that you don't like or if you hear something negative about a colleague from a parent, intern, or church member—don't listen. Redirect the complainer to take his or her concern or issue back to the person involved. If you have a problem with a coworker, handle it in person. Face to face. Email and Facebook are terrible ways to handle conflict. Unless there is some type of toxic abuse or severe mismanagement going on that endangers others, don't bring in a ministry supervisor until you've exhausted all other possibilities.

My one (and so far only) fallout with a male coworker (see

chapter 6) could have been avoided if things had been handled face to face from the start. If our department head had directed my male coworker to handle his grievances directly with me in person…things would have been so much better.

## WE ARE PARTNERS IN MINISTRY

Sometimes our gender impacts how we relate to one another. After a particularly frustrating week of ministry, I asked to meet with my boss, a man whom I greatly respect. I needed to vent, and I hoped he might have some insights into my problem. Instead of giving me advice, he told me, "You internalize things too much. Just let it go." Moments later, he left my office, no doubt thinking he'd handled the situation well. I, on the other hand, closed the door and cried.

Situations like these have taught me much about working with men:

- If I cry in a meeting, my male colleagues will stop seeing me as their peer and instead, start trying to protect me.

- Men hear and respond better to questions rather than outright disagreement.

- Male colleagues aren't the best people to vent to because it's typically their nature to problem solve rather than just listen.

Men and women think differently, relate to one another differently, and do ministry differently. That's why we need both men and women in ministry. Having finally come to this conclusion, I recently invited that same male pastor to join our youth group on a retreat. He willingly agreed, even though doing so meant missing worship with our congregation. He participated in our retreat programming and led worship for my students. I watched in awe at how the teens responded to him.

That's when I realized that even though working with men can, at times, be frustrating, our male colleagues aren't actually our enemies. They're our partners in ministry.

— *Jen Bradbury*

Heather Lea Campbell is a youth worker who blogs and friend in youth ministry. She has three helpful tips to share about working with men in youth ministry:

### 1. Realize that women really are different from men—and that's okay!

God made men and women in his image, and both genders have beautiful characteristics that should remind each other of God. For example, women tend to be more nurturing and sensitive. This is something you should celebrate! Use those strengths, mixed with your male colleagues' strengths, to create a ministry environment that works.

This also translates to other areas. Women aren't necessarily interested in the same things guys are. For instance, not all women saw the latest Iron Man movie, and they sure don't want to spend an entire staff meeting talking about it. (Okay, well some do.) Women may be more limited physically (especially if they're pregnant). Help the guys you work with to consider these things when they're doing program planning. And let them know that if they're ever unsure about your physical capabilities, they should just ask!

### 2. Don't limit your identity to being "the woman."

Don't allow men to bring up the fact that you're a woman all the time. It's annoying! Sure, we're different from one another. But if you're having an emotional day, don't let the guys write it off as you having a "chick moment" or talk about you (or other women) as PMSing. Men can have emotional moments too, right?

Sometimes I feel like I get boxed in because I'm a woman—I can only work with girls, write about girls, and talk about girls. It's like all I have to contribute to the ministry is the fact that I'm a woman. And while I love that I'm a rarity in youth ministry, I want my male colleagues to celebrate *all* that I have to offer. I love talking to and about young women, but it's not all that I am. We are more than our genders—we are bearers of the image of God. So I seek to be all things to all people, not confined to one part of my identity.

### 3. Realize every woman is different.

There are great women who love baking and doing arts and crafts. That's great! Those skills are needed. But there are other women who can preach a killer sermon or lead an awesome dodgeball game. Some may be dainty; others are athletic. Just like men have different characteristics, so do women! Some women you can tease like a sister; others want to be treated like a professional. Let men know how you want to be treated, especially if being treated like their little sister isn't what you desire.

## CO-PASTORING

What if you're working side-by-side with a male youth pastor? Hannah Stevens has six helpful tips for a co-pastoring scenario:

1. Don't feel like you have to do and be good at everything. You and your co-pastor will have different talents, perspectives, and ideas. That's probably why you were both hired.

2. Spend time getting to know where you and your co-pastor each excel. It's helpful to take note of the gifts he has that you don't, and vice versa. Rather than trying to prove yourself, become aware and grateful for what you each bring to the ministry.

3. Find ways to lean in to your talents to improve the ministry.

4. Be diplomatic in how you divide the less desirable tasks and try to split them as evenly as possible.

5. It's also important, when possible, to fight each other's battles. It will help you feel like a team, and it will keep your

emotions in check when your co-pastor is standing up for the thing you believe in, and vice versa.

6. It's not a competition. You and your co-pastor have to be a team.

My final suggestion for having a good working relationship with your male colleagues is have fun! Let those foam finger rockets fly. Play harmless practical jokes on one another. Having fun together is powerful. When you have fun, you're really saying, "I like working with you." And when you like working with someone, it's so much easier to communicate well and advocate for one another. When you like someone, you're less likely to call her bossy behind her back or be

## HAVE FUN

In my opinion, the worst thing about working with men in youth ministry is how often they eat! Within one weekend, I think we went to Chick-fil-A five times. I think youth ministry may be the hardest career field in which to honor your body. But working with your brothers in Christ is always interesting. In our office we're big fans of Nerf guns. Whether we're shooting at each other when we're stressed or shooting unsuspecting students when they arrive, we love to have fun. For example, my boss hates cats, so what could be better than hiding cat memorabilia throughout his office? Months later, I'm still getting texts whenever he finds a cat in a drawer or behind a book!

Guys are weird, and they eat a lot, and sometimes they smell; but they're a lot of fun. Find the good aspects of working with them. And when one of them asks you to send an email for him, kindly remind him that you're not his assistant (unless, of course, you help run admin!). They'll get it eventually. Most men won't get their feelings hurt if you stand up for yourself. So stand up for yourself when needed and don't be afraid to have some fun at work!

— *Chelsea Peddecord*

afraid to talk with him about the important things that matter. I do love keeping those foam finger rockets in my desk and launching them at coworkers every chance I get.

# QUESTIONS FOR REFLECTION

1. What do you enjoy about partnering with the opposite gender in youth ministry?

2. What do wish were easier about partnering with the opposite gender in youth ministry?

3. How might fun and practical jokes help communication and team chemistry?

4. What is your deepest pain or greatest joy in serving on a youth ministry team with other men and women?

5. How can you leverage your strengths and staff around your weaknesses to create a more optimal ministry team?

6. What one thing could you do better when it comes to working on a ministry team with the opposite sex?

7. Have you ever cried in front of a male colleague or ministry volunteer? How did he handle that? Did you feel good about it or embarrassed by it?

8. How can being yourself, emotions and all, be an asset to team ministry?

9. Action Step: Think of something you appreciate about each of the guys you work or volunteer with and then *tell them.*

# 8

# CUP O' NOODLE (ALONE)

*Love isn't hard to spot at a distance; it usually looks like our friends running towards us when we've failed again.*

— Love Does Twitter Feed (@lovedoes)

I'm driving my Ford Escape to one of those large hobby stores while my one-year-old is strapped comfortably in her car seat munching on Cheerios. Blasting Taylor Swift's *Red* and running youth ministry errands, I am on my way to pick up something for a youth group project I'm working on. As I drive down a four-lane freeway in San Diego on a sunny afternoon, something unexpected happens. A tan minivan in front of me turns on its left blinker. The driver of the Toyota Sienna looks over her shoulder and proceeds to change lanes. But at the last moment, before an almost collision, she notices a car in her blind spot. Instead of returning gently to her lane, she freaks out and turns her wheel sharply to avoid the car she's about to sideswipe.

Well, you can probably guess what happens next. She loses control of her minivan. And as she continues to swerve and overcorrect, the situation only gets worse. Her car spins uncontrollably across all four lanes of freeway traffic. This is all happening just a few yards in front of me. I slow down as soon as I notice her overcorrecting and put as much distance between my vehicle and the out-of-control minivan as I possibly can. I pray she doesn't spin into anyone else, and I am freaking out because she might slam into my car. There is little I can do. I stop, turn on my hazards, and pray everyone behind me is paying attention. I hope no approaching cars slam into me as I'm now stopped on the freeway and trying to stay the heck out of the way. You can imagine my concern, especially with my young daughter in the car.

The minivan swerves and spins from the far left side of the freeway to the far right, going up an embankment, rolling over, and eventually landing upright with all tires safely on the ground. Looking only slightly banged up and remarkably intact, the Sienna seems practically unscathed. It makes me want to buy a minivan. No other cars are hit, and for a moment I'm unsure what to do. Rattled and feeling anxious because it all happened within a matter of seconds, I pull off the freeway with my hazard lights still on. I reach for my cell phone and wonder if I need to call 911 or check on the people in the van. I don't want to leave my one-year-old. I pray someone else will come to the rescue so I can get off the side of the freeway.

I notice several other people stop right away. Another minivan quickly pulls over right in front of me, and a female exits the passenger side. She runs toward the Sienna and heads up the embankment as quickly as she can. A man, who is probably the woman's husband, gets out on the driver's side. He's speaking to someone on his cell phone. They seem to know the people in the Sienna. By the looks on their faces, I can tell they are running toward friends, not strangers. Running to help.

*They must be caravanning somewhere*, I think to myself. I pray there are no injuries and no children in the van. When I notice everything is being taken care of, I leave the scene so I can get my baby away from the situation.

Crashes, accidents, and hurtful collisions happen on the freeway, in life, in relationships, in ministry, in marriage, and in parenting. Sometimes you crash or get hurt or collide with disaster because you miss something in a blind spot. Maybe you foolishly head into a bad situation, marital mismatch, or ministry mistake. Occasionally you may be tempted to overcorrect into something worse. Maybe you turn on your blinker and veer into the left lane when you should pause a moment longer to look over your shoulder before changing course.

Friends, family, and ministry volunteers traveling through life and ministry with us often see what we don't see. They see our blind spots because they're traveling ahead of us, beside us, and behind us. When disaster, depression, discouragement, or despair strikes, they come running. The question is, when you find yourself bent out of shape and sitting upright after an unexpected rollover on a weekday afternoon, do you have friends who come running to your rescue?

As a woman in youth ministry, sometimes I've found this to be an awkward reality to live in—particularly during lunchtime in the office. I'm not a 19-year-old youth intern anymore. I'm also not one of the guys or a male pastor on staff. I don't long for lunches talking about basketball games and fantasy football, nor do I have a lot of stay-at-home mom friends to meet for lunch. My work schedule puts me on a different track and time schedule than most of my mom friends. And after recently moving away from San Diego where I've lived my *entire* life, I don't have many friends period. (Not yet...but that's changing fast!)

I remember a few years ago as I was sitting in my windowless office, I could hear all the guy pastors leaving for a "boys only" pastoral lunch meeting. All the young college youth interns were off to lunch with whomever they were dating at the time

If you ask anyone in ministry, they've struggled with loneliness. When you begin in youth ministry, adults treat you like another daughter. Then you reach an age where everyone around you is married with kids, and eventually you're surrounded by young and eager (and slightly more energetic) interns. There will be a point when you need your girls! Community is something beautiful and essential for spiritual life. Find these people, go to a conference, ask women from another church out to lunch, make it happen! Just don't get pizza because I'm sure you've eaten that several times this month already. Go make friends because nothing is more fun than loving the Lord with people by your side.

—*Chelsea Peddecord*

or heading out to finish homework before a class. My outgoing admin assistant usually had lunch plans with friends or had to cover breaks for other admins. Most of the church staff had offices across the street or on the other side of long hallways and closed doors. So there I was. Alone in my office with a Cup O' Noodle.

I remember how pathetic that was. If you've ever tried to navigate lunchtime in any workplace, you know it can be a little like high school. You're either in or you're out. I am not one to be left out or be okay with the status quo. So I did something about it. I realized I had to be proactive. I am by no means an extrovert, but I am *very goal oriented.* So my new goal was to stop eating Cup O' Noodle alone in my office. I decided then and there to make lunchtime matter. Of course I have those days, like you do, where I'm so busy working on a project that I don't eat lunch at all. Or there are days when I'm busy visiting schools or meeting with youth volunteers. But on those days when it seems like everyone (except you) is off somewhere having lunch, you might wonder, *Gee, who are my people? Why am I alone with a Cup O' Noodle?*

My first piece of advice is to champion for a communal space in the office where people can eat together and play together. Most churches don't think strategically about their office spaces and fail to design them with community and collaboration in mind. If everyone has an office behind a closed door and there isn't a central space dedicated to eating, brewing coffee, and spending time together, you're only perpetuating a "keep them separated" sterile office environment. So of course guy pastors go out to eat with other guy pastors. Interns stick with interns. Children's ministry staff stay on their side of the building. And you rarely ever co-mingle with anyone, especially the higher-ups. That's boring. But worse than that, it squashes creativity, collaboration, community, and teamwork.

In a youth ministry age where we push for intergenerational Sticky Faith experiences,[27] it would make sense to emulate that ideal Monday through Friday within the church office too. Advocate and dream for a more creative and effective office environment. If you haven't seen Google's New York office yet, do a Google search for "Google Office Space" and prepare to be blown away.[28]

The church where I work now has brilliantly done away with separate office spaces. They purposefully created an environment that fosters creativity, collaboration, and community. All of the children's and student ministry staff, along with other departments in the church, work out in the open in hip, nicely designed cubicles so we can see each other, interact, and collaborate. And the few who need private offices because they do a lot of counseling, extensive teaching prep, and closed-door meetings do have their own offices. But most do *not*.

On my first day on the job, I found a sweet set of noise-canceling headphones on my desk. Everyone gets those here. We also have ample meeting rooms and counseling offices available for those times when we need to talk privately, run a meeting, or use the phone without everyone overhearing our conversation. (And these spaces double as youth ministry small group spaces...ding ding ding!) Working in a space designed for interaction and interruption fuels creativity and fast-tracks community. Plus, we've got giant dry erase boards and Apple products everywhere. Plenty of space and surfaces to document the latest great idea. And bad ones too.

At 4:55 p.m. at the end of the workweek, with only five minutes left until the weekend, one of our high school pastors busts out the weekend Spotify play mix for a little celebration dance party before heading home. It's a place where we work hard but we also work hard *together*. A place committed to wholeness, journey, community, roots, and celebration. A place that intentionally infuses all of those things into the working environment. What is genius is they really did design the office space with community in mind.

You can't avoid anyone if you want a coffee refill. It's a place where everyone from the executive staff, to the teaching pastor, to the graphic designer, to the nursery director will come to fill their coffee mugs, put away their lunches, and connect with each other. It's a space designed with *mingling in mind*, where equality is not just a word but a reality as we all exist together in the same space. The guy pastors. The girl pastors. Those in leadership. Those in support positions. There is no assigned senior pastor parking space. You feel like you're all on the same team and valued as an owner/expert of your own ministry area as you work separately yet together for the same mission of *"Living out the way of Jesus in missional communities, announcing the arrival of his kingdom, working for measurable change among the oppressed."*[29]

An intentional community environment breeds real community experiences. Often at lunchtime, someone will walk over and say, *"I'm going to go eat in the cafe area. If you haven't eaten, do you want to join us?"* It's so different than my old Cup O' Noodle world. You become what you're exposed to.

> One of the biggest blessings in my life has been my friendships with other pastors and youth pastors in the area. In my denomination we're discouraged against maintaining close relationships with people in the congregation once we've ended a call at a particular church. Having other friends in ministry gives me people who know the bigger story of my life. They're the ones I can be real with regarding challenges in a particular setting, and they give me new ideas since their churches do things differently than mine does. We make time to get together for a meal and fellowship twice a month. I invite them to my home—they bring parts of the meal and help clean up! Their laughter and camaraderie has been invaluable!
>
> — *Carmen Garrigan*

Most of us don't work at Google or at churches who think about office space too much. Gee…how many churches even have office spaces these days? So how do you create community, build relationships, and find "your people" when being alone with a Cup O' Noodle is so much easier? Are you taking the initiative to extend an invitation to mingle when it's easier to hide away and play Candy Crush? Do you walk toward people, or do you hide in your office with a granola bar? Whether your church is large or small, I challenge you to get out of your chair. Get off your phone or computer and mingle. Don't eat lunch at your desk. Sit with your lunch or Cup O' Noodle out in the open and invite others to the table.

## FINDING FEMALE FRIENDS IN YOUTH MINISTRY

When I lived in San Diego, I was blessed to have a couple of youth ministry friends that I got to hang out with—Christina and Tina. Somehow, unbeknownst to me, God orchestrated our lives to overlap on multiple levels. They provided friendships that I really needed as well as professional support. And they saw me through some pretty rough times in youth ministry. We first got to know each other through a few mutual ministry partnerships, but mostly by being a part of our local youth ministry network.

I'm always kind of amazed by how much the three of us have in common. First, we are all doing *middle school ministry*. You know this takes a special kind of person. We all disappointed our parents by choosing youth ministry as our careers; it's a full-time job for us all. Of course, we're all females in youth ministry, we wear makeup, and we require large amounts of chocolate, carbs, and girl time.

To make these friendships even sweeter—and to prove that God brought all of us into this friendship for a purpose—our kids attended the same charter school. We got to high-five each other in the carpool line each school day. This is a school with a long waiting list and a lottery to get in, and there we all were. Together. You'd think our lives couldn't possibly have more in common, but then we all had babies within three months of each other. (No, we didn't plan it. But it's still pretty cool, huh?)

Do you have female friends in youth ministry? If not, you need to pray and ask God to bring you some. Every female in youth ministry needs the friendship, support, and understanding of the rare few who do what we do. For my friends and me, we have lives that are full and exhausting from babies waking us up at dawn to late nights working on youth talks. We all have kids with homework, a full-time focus on youth ministry, and everyday responsibilities like dinner, dishes, bath time, and husbands to love and feed. I need time with women who understand all that I am juggling.

I need friends who know what it's like to be female in the very male world of professional ministry. I need friends who will listen to my fears and insecurities and understand the challenges of being female in youth ministry. We need a safe and understanding place to share all the things you can't tweet, blog, or talk to church friends about because "I work here."

These women are my lifelines on days when I hit bottom and begin searching job postings on *ChurchStaffing.com* because, you know, the grass is always greener on the other side.

I need these adult friends in my life, and they need me. As a woman in youth ministry, I hope you take the time to seek out these kinds of friendships. Look for them, pray for them, beg God for them. Be vulnerable, show up at Panera even though there's a good chance everyone else may be too busy and bail on you at the last minute. Show up anyway! God will wow your socks off. He has friends in mind for you. Deep, lasting friendships with women can be hard to find. They take time and effort like any good relationship does.

Do not give up on the gift of friendship. Cultivate it. Be purposeful. Be intentional. My friendships with these women came to be when I was least expecting it, and when I really needed them the most. I was feeling youth ministry friendless, longing for strong friendships with women in youth ministry who lived locally. I needed someone I could meet at Starbucks and speak candidly with that person. And God gave me Christina and Tina.

When we became friends, it was unclear how long the three of us would be doing youth ministry within a 10-mile radius of one another. Two years or ten? How long will our kids all be in the same school? We knew we wouldn't always be able to bring our babies on play dates as we talked about campus ministry and student small groups. As my friend Christina said, "For a season we have each other, and we need to take advantage of it." I hope you will too.

Six months later, Christina moved to the Los Angeles area, and then I moved out of state shortly after that. Yet, I'm still grateful for these friendships and for the time I invested into them. I know these two women are only one video chat or text away.

# QUESTIONS FOR REFLECTION

1. How do you cultivate female friendships in youth ministry?

2. Who are "your people"—the friends you can turn to who are unimpressed by any perceived "coolness" about you or your job accomplishments. Do you have people you can be real with?

3. What can you do this week to be more intentional in getting to know those you work or serve with?

4. Have you ever felt left out as a female youth pastor?

5. If you work on staff in a church, what is your office space like? Does it help or hinder communication and collaboration?

6. How can you be vulnerable this week or this month and put yourself out there to meet other women who work or volunteer in ministry like you do?

7. Pray. Pray for eyes to see and to notice potential friendships. Pray for courage to extend a lunch invitation or to show up somewhere where you can meet other women in youth ministry.

8. Action Step: Eat lunch out in the open. If you're at work, don't hide at your desk. Find a spot in a lobby or a shared space. If you're working from home all week, invite someone over to eat lunch with you.

# 9

# SHE'S LEADING MEN (LETTING YOUNGER LEADERS AND VOLUNTEERS LEAD)

Leading men and people a lot older than you can feel unnatural sometimes. Particularly if it's something you're not used to observing in your church (let's change that, okay?) or are never allowed to do. Many (but not all) women lack the tools, training, and support to lead comfortably in those settings where men typically lead. This is especially true if you attended a more conservative Bible college or grew up in a more conservative evangelical home.

My undergraduate ministry degree came from a Christian college in Southern California that leans heavily away from female Bible teachers. I call those years my "Left Behind days." (Tim LaHaye, coauthor of the Left Behind series, was one of the Bible college's founders.) No one told me I'd enrolled in the Concerned Women for America[30] college or helped me discern my own theology for women in ministry leadership. But it wasn't a huge concern for me back then because there was no shortage of youth ministry to be done, and I was loving my internship at a large Southern Baptist church doing more ministry than I'd ever dreamed of doing.

I've spent many a year as either a female youth intern or working with female interns and volunteers in a supervisory role. I've had the opportunity to spend a few Sundays observing a youth program in a local church where Mariah Sherman, a former female youth intern of mine, is now leading the entire student ministry, including a dozen or so volunteers. Half of her team is older than she is, and more than half of them are men. Watching her lead is a beautiful thing. I love to see what happens when a younger youth leader is unleashed into a full-fledged youth ministry of her own. A few things came to mind as I observed a multitude of exciting things that God is doing in this youth ministry led by a 22-year-old female.

First, when the sky is the limit, the sky *really* is the limit. Mariah's church (which is Southern Baptist) is open to new ideas and supportive of women in pastoral leadership. It's a beautiful church doing great work. What I love is how this particular church will go to great lengths to reach unchurched teenagers. When a church strategically makes Sunday mornings feel less foreign to those who have no church experience, cool things happen. Less churchy, more relational. More comfortable. Thus, there is a ton of openness and an opportunity for this young youth leader to try new things, lean in to her leadership, and really use those gifts to do whatever

Let's address the elephant in the room: A certain percentage of men are never going to accept your leadership within the church. I don't like it, but there it is. They aren't evil. They don't hate you. And they aren't the enemy. Remember that. You probably aren't going to have to address the issue of leading these men because, unfortunately, they won't choose to be on your team.

My experience has been that almost everyone is looking for people to pour into them. They are looking for someone who will care for them, who will serve them, who will offer kindness and support. Men and women alike need this, and if you are a strong and gracious leader, they will look to you. I think we lead by putting others first and loving them well; our team members, men and women, can respect and get behind that.

—*Heather Henderson*

she wants. To be able to lead as a young female in youth ministry without the confines of supervisors, gender bias, or "this is how we do it here"—her leadership soared.

As I watched Mariah lead, I was dazzled, impressed, and excited to see what can be done when limitations and "we've always done it this way" traditions are removed. It was exciting to see a talented young female youth worker get launched into a ministry all her own. She was working at a forward-thinking Baptist church with a much more egalitarian work environment that showed little resistance to "out of the box" ideas.

After visiting the church, my 11-year-old commented, "Wow, Mom! They do a lot here that people get grumpy about at our old church." He was quite taken by this newfound freedom. Not that our home church was super restrictive... okay, never mind. They totally were. Granted, they have a different target audience on Sunday mornings, but even so, the contrast was huge. Little differences like Monster energy drinks and Starbucks Frappuccinos being given to visitors. Rap music—even non-Christian rap (gasp!)—Taylor Swift, and Coldplay music was playing in the youth room. People were skateboarding across the floor, and a *ton* of noise blasting from the youth room. But no one seemed to be bothered by the crazy loudness of it all. Is that Halo being played on the video game system? Yes. My 11-year-old was all smiles.

Every church is different and has to pay attention to the demographics and culture of the target audience they're trying to reach, making sure it also meshes well with the vision of the church leadership. So I'm not saying this is a ministry style you have to follow, nor necessarily should. What struck me is that Mariah has the support of her church leadership to run free. They trust her. Plus, it was working, and working really well! Watching her have great freedom to strategically try new things is so fun! If you sit down with her, she can give you a crystal clear strategy for why they do what they do on a Sunday morning, and quite frankly, it is compelling and genius.

Instead of primarily keeping a bunch of conservative parents happy while trying to reach students (which is the environment I'd formerly been in), her goal is simply to reach unchurched teens. That changes everything. She frames her ministry and her leadership through the lens of reaching unchurched students while empowering Christian students to live and share their faith.

I saw firsthand what can happen when younger leaders run free—they do what you've been doing all along, but they do it *even better.* One thing that had sunk to a B-minus level in my own ministry was student leadership. Not that I wasn't doing a good job; I was just too busy running middle school small groups, lesson planning, and doing a lot of campus ministry. When too much is on your plate, sometimes you inadvertently let things slide.

When a church empowers younger leaders to lead, maybe they take your B-minuses to an A+. There are no cheesy student leader acronyms (SALT, anyone?), but the student staff meeting is held before each service and the teens have specific responsibilities each week. I was able to partake in her student staff team meeting to run through the Sunday morning agenda, and then they met again after the service to recap and plan for next week. It's what we've been doing all along, only better. I began to wonder why I hadn't put younger ministry staff completely in charge of the student leadership already. Maybe because they too have too much on their plates, as tons of ministry responsibilities are also on their shoulders.

So here's the question for those of you who have younger female ministry staff and volunteers: Do you allow room in your ministry to give away leadership? Do you empower your female volunteers and staff to lead? Do you let them preach and lead just as much as the guys do? If you lead a ministry with young interns or college-age volunteers, equip them to lead now. Don't wait. Why train them only to see them achieve their optimal impact once they *leave* your ministry context? Give them tons of space and your blessing to run free and try new things while they are with your ministry. Girls starting out in youth ministry need experience leading those who are older than them and younger than them, and they need opportunities to figure out how to lead men who might not always be comfortable having a female in charge.

Give away your ministry. Empower others to lead. This is especially a must if you're an older youth worker. The youthfulness, positive attitude, new ideas, and untainted zest for youth ministry of your younger volunteers will only make you better. Your experience, knowledge of what your church culture is okay with (or not okay with), and input will only make them better. Mutual mentoring is happening here. I mentor Mariah just as much as she mentors me! Sure, interns or young volunteers might fall flat on their faces with a terrible idea, but what if it turns out to be the next best thing you've ever done? Protect their time and give them room to shine.

It's hard to be awesome when you're too busy. If you lead a team of young volunteers or interns, ask yourself if your team is too busy with the mundane. Make sure they aren't completely bogged down with less fruitful ministry jobs. Things like handing out VBS flyers, cleaning up rat poop under the youth room sofas, stuffing 2,000-piece mailers, and helping out every other ministry because "you've got youth volunteers to spare" can stifle the time they have to do real ministry.

One time our team of middle school volunteers couldn't help with a middle school Halloween dance at the local public school because they were too busy helping at an event our children's ministry was hosting. They were too busy to be middle school youth workers at the middle school. If you want them to lead well, let them lean fully into their volunteer roles without making them fill holes in other ministries.

Be a team player, but not always at the expense of your own ministry. Not that those church mailers, children's outreach events, picking up trash after an event, or other church-wide helping things are bad. They might not even be things you can cut. But if you can, protect the wiggle room in your volunteers' schedules. Honestly evaluate your ministry context and ask: Can my volunteers and staff try new things? Can they spend more time *with* students and less time picking up trash? Give young ministry volunteers freedom to dream youth ministry dreams and be unleashed for maximum kingdom impact. It might knock your socks off. The best ministry is the ministry you empower someone else to do.

Let young leaders grow by visiting other youth groups at least once or twice a year. Learning from other leaders is a huge benefit to your own ministry. This is especially helpful for young female youth interns and volunteers. Let them see how other female youth pastors lead men, teach boys, work with parents, and lead those who are older or a lot younger than they are. It's sooo worth it. All youth workers need to get out of their "we've always done it this way" rut and be inspired by the

Relational ministry is bae. If you haven't heard the term *bae* before, it stands for "before anything else." Relational ministry is so incredibly important. We can plan events and preach awesome sermons all day long, but relationships are what make everything click. Especially when you're working with those who are older than you. I'm college age, so I definitely understand this struggle. Meeting with volunteers may seem tiresome, but I'm a big believer in the idea that teens, parents, and volunteers are equally important. And making time to get to know them can make everything go much smoother. So equip your leaders. When a team loves their coach, everyone plays better. You should never be too busy to learn from and love on those around you.

— *Chelsea Peddecord*

great ideas out there. See what other ministries are doing and keep it fresh.

One question I get asked a lot by female youth ministry workers and volunteers who are just beginning in youth ministry is how to lead men and how to lead others who are a lot older than you. I asked Mariah Sherman, the young 20-something youth pastor I just told you about, to share some tips. Here's what she had to say:

You're young—strike one.
You're a woman—strike two.
You look like a 16-year-old—strike three.

Okay, maybe you don't have that last problem, but I certainly do! Here are some tips on being a young woman in leadership.

**1. Hone in on the vision for your ministry.**
- Hint: It's probably a student-friendly version of the larger church vision.

- Lots of things are great, but stick to what furthers the vision.

**2. Know why you do things.**
- It's hard for your volunteers to take you seriously when it feels like you're "flying by the seat of your pants"—and especially when they expect you to do this because of your age and gender.

- If there is no purpose to an activity or event that furthers the goal behind what you're doing, scratch it and do something else.

- Sell your volunteers on the *why* behind everything. This will transform your volunteers from a-group-that-listens-to-you-because-they-love-Jesus into a *team* working toward a goal. Also, it will help them develop respect for your leadership and take you more seriously.

### 3. *Don't* act your age.

- Because you are young, parents and volunteers will expect you to be disorganized and unprofessional. This problem is compounded when people attach words to you like *adorable* and *cute* instead of *competent* and *respectable*. Don't prove them right.

- Show up early, stay late.

- Find people to keep in your close circle that will help you see the perspectives, interests, and concerns of the parents, middle-aged volunteers, and men on your staff.

### 4. Be organized!

- You have to stay twice as organized as the 35-year-old male pastor you replaced if you want to receive half the respect and trust he got. It's sad, but true.

- Plan six months in advance and keep things planned way ahead.

- Before an event or program time, take five minutes to think through the day and make sure your i's are dotted and your t's are crossed.

If you're the designated youth pastor at your church, you will most likely be teaching both male and female students on a regular basis. Whether from the stage during a youth program, or in a Sunday school class, or during a small informal summer Bible study, it's likely you'll be asked to teach guys and girls. And sometimes well-meaning people will question whether or not that's okay.

A few days ago, I received this email from a young female who's just starting out in youth ministry:

> *Hey Gina!*
> *I am ecstatic to be nearing graduation. I am finishing my last semester of college in May. I am graduating.*

*I am passionate about student ministry, and I have learned so much that I cannot wait to implement. I have been hired as a full-time youth pastor. I interned two summers in a row at the church that offered me the full-time paid position.*

*Knowing the huge weight of this position, I sought out one of my youth ministry professors after class today and told him about the opportunity I've been given. I asked him for insight and guidance in how to go about speaking in a way that is effective and relatable to both teenage boys and teenage girls.*

*His response was that I should not have that task. He stated that I could be a great overseer and director of the ministry, but I should never be teaching [men] on a regular basis.*

*I am at a loss as to what to do. I will strive to recruit male volunteers who can help teach, but is it my place not to teach until that time comes? How did you make it work as a female youth pastor in your 20s? I would love to gain some of your insights and perspectives on student ministry.*[31]

I've received many emails like this. A female who is interested in youth ministry has a conversation with a pastor, college professor, or concerned individual who asks, "So how are you going to reach the guys?" Or even worse, they tell her, "You shouldn't be leading or teaching teenage boys." Oftentimes these now disillusioned and discouraged women will then frantically Google WOMEN IN YOUTH MINISTRY, and that's how they find my blog.

What bothers me the most about this youth ministry professor's response is that no one ever wonders if male pastors can reach and effectively teach girls.

The first time I ever spoke, I gave my testimony to 500 middle school students. Now here's what I think: Anyone can tell her story; anyone can tell about what Jesus is doing in her life. Are there some women who struggle to work with boys? Absolutely. Are there men who struggle to work with girls? Absolutely. AND THAT'S OKAY! We are differently gifted. But Jesus did something in my life, and I can share that story with whomever I want, whether that person is male or female. It's simply their choice to listen. I love preaching to both genders and speaking gives me joy. Sure, I preach a little differently if it's only girls. But that's okay because speaking has a lot to do with knowing your audience. Are there any real reasons for girls not to be in youth ministry? No. So whether I'm called a "middle school coordinator," a "girls minister," or even a "middle school girls coordinator," my job title doesn't stop the work of God. I can do ministry differently than a man can do ministry. The more we choose to work together, the more our King is glorified.

— *Chelsea Peddecord*

When asked how I reach guys and relate to them as a female in youth ministry, I have a few candid answers:

## 1. I relate to the guys the same way male youth pastors relate to the girls.

I wasn't hindered or harmed by having male youth pastors when I was a teenager. It made no difference to me. Truth is truth and God's Word is powerful. It doesn't matter if it's a girl or a guy preaching it. God's Word and the Holy Spirit speak into the lives of students regardless of a youth worker's gender. It's important to hire someone who is skilled, called, and capable of reaching teens. Gender is irrelevant. And why doesn't anyone ask the same question if a *guy* is preaching every weekend to females? No one seems concerned about how he relates to girls!

**2. As a paid youth worker, I've always believed in team ministry.**

I may not have had the benefit of female youth workers or female youth volunteers during my own youth group days, but I certainly believe in a team ministry approach. I make sure to have both male and female staff on our teams. Old and young, married and single, trendy and nerdy. Parents of teens, and newlyweds without kids. Students need a variety of adults invested in their lives. It's not up to one gender or one ultra-cool hipster youth leader. Variety is essential. One person cannot relate well to every kid anyway. I may be female, but that doesn't mean I'm going to automatically connect with every girl in my ministry. A teen girl might be into guitar, volleyball, and water polo, and I am the least likely person to have anything in common with that!

**3. It's the married couples with kids who impacted my life the most.**

I'm not saying you have to be married and have kids to be effective, but you should be intentional about having married couples and parents integrated into your youth ministry. As a youth pastor, make it a priority to create opportunities for married couples in your church to enfold and invite the teenagers among them into the community.

Baby-sitting for my Campus Life director and his wife allowed me to experience youth ministry through the context of family. Going on youth ministry trips with them to baby-sit their kids gave me a glimpse into what I wanted my future to look like. It made a lifelong impression on me, giving me a yearning to one day be that kind of a family—a family who welcomes teenagers into the everyday rhythm of family life in a Jesus-loving home. I saw them parent. I saw them do youth ministry. I saw them go through personal loss. I was able to eat at their kitchen table and accompany them on Campus Life trips. Having a front row seat to watch a happily married couple raise kids together is something the guys and girls in your youth group need desperately. So many of our teens come from crappy family situations, and they need to see what healthy looks like.

**4. Staff around strengths and weaknesses, not gender.**
Let's be honest. Not everyone is great at speaking in front of teenagers. So I tend to care less about a teacher's gender and more about content and their overall effectiveness as a speaker. Just because someone is male or female doesn't necessarily mean he or she will connect with the audience. Especially if that person happens to suck at speaking. If your skill set is teaching, take every opportunity to teach and grow in your talent. If you bring in guest teachers, do it because you want to empower your volunteers to use their gifts. Don't do it because of their gender.

Okay, this is going to sound a little arrogant, but it's honest. At one of the churches where I used to work, the middle schoolers *always* preferred my teaching. My gift is speaking/teaching and it comes naturally to me. My male co-worker at the time? Not so much. He really struggled with it. It wasn't his area of strength, but it was a major part of his job description because he was the male youth leader. As the youth pastor, he spoke three out of four Sundays. As a ministry associate, I was allowed to teach once a month. If we'd staffed around our strengths instead of our genders, everyone could have thrived in their area of giftedness, and the entire ministry would have benefited.

# QUESTIONS FOR REFLECTION

1. Leading men. Teaching boys. Whether you're young or older and not as cool as you used to be, how do you lead the guys in your ministry?

2. Read 1 Timothy 4:12. What tips do you have for those who are leading a team of adults who are a lot older than they are?

3. Do you get to use your gifts and strengths in your current ministry context?

4. Do you think anyone ever wonders how all of those guy pastors reach and effectively teach girls?

5. What tips and ideas do you have for reaching the boys in your youth ministry?

6. Who has impacted your spiritual life the most? Were they male or female? Was it a married couple? Was it a variety of people?

7. Why is team ministry vital to reaching the teens in your church?

# 10

## THE PILL, PRESBYS, AND PAYCHECKS

### THE PILL

When I first got out of college, I worked at a Southern Baptist Convention (SBC) church as a full-time youth director with no benefits. I didn't think too much about health insurance at the time because this church didn't provide health insurance for anyone on staff. Young and excited to get a paycheck of any kind, I figured I'd worry about it later. However, while it struck me as odd that the church provided the senior pastor (a male) and the associate pastor (a male) with extra money to get their own health insurance plans, it didn't really bother me. I knew these two men had families to provide for, and I did not. (Not yet, anyway.)

As a newlywed, I was hopeful that my husband would one day find a job with health insurance. But at that point he was working part time as a waiter and finishing up his teaching credential. I wish someone had told me back then how having health insurance and affordable access to birth control positively impacts women in the workforce.

An article studying the economic benefits of a woman's ability to determine whether and when to have children, points out that:

> *A number of economic studies have examined the impact of contraceptive access on women's participation in the workforce. Similar to those studies looking at educational achievement, one body of evidence focuses on how women's professional pursuits and the amount of time they spent in the paid labor force evolved as state statutes made the pill legally accessible to young, unmarried women around 1970.*[32]

My advice for young women who are beginning their careers in paid vocational ministry is to seriously think about health insurance, birth control, and when and how many children you want to have someday. Don't assume you can deal with those issues later just because you don't currently have a family to support. A conversation with a mentor or a female clergy member about birth control, health insurance, and adequate compensation would have been so helpful to me as a young woman just starting out in youth ministry.

Are you ready for some real advice that hardly anyone will be brave enough to give you? Protect yourself sexually. I'm not afraid to say it's dumb to assume single women (and men) will always make perfect decisions when it comes to their sexuality and remain abstinent until marriage. Although I hope they truly practice what they preach. Yes, you could go "Duggar" and choose to be chaperoned on your dates until you get married, thereby establishing really great boundaries to protect yourself from sexual temptation. That would be awesome. But for the rest of us who are prone to moments of human frailty, be careful about what you assume could never happen. Even in the most conservative evangelical environments, we all know couples who've "oopsed" in this area or simply chose to lie to everyone about it. Most pretend to wait until marriage while the reality is that very few obtain the ideal we all hope for. To be clear, it's an ideal I still firmly believe in. I'm a mom of a 12-year-old boy, after all. Courting looks better and better every day.

I've worked with enough youth ministry interns and Christian college students who claim to be "waiting until marriage" to know it's not often the case. In fact, it's rarely the case. One full-time youth ministry volunteer I was working with in a "True Love Waits" purity ring kind of a church told me how almost every intern had confided in her that they'd been having sex during their student ministry internship with their soon-to-be husband or wife. Of course, they didn't own up to it until well after they were married with kids. Christians may know it's God's best for them to wait, yet still opt to secretly mess around. Sexual purity in today's world is a difficult reality to live in, and we need to be honest about it instead of pretending to be what we're not.

Men who stumble or make a mistake sexually can usually move on with life and continue in their call to ministry. Oftentimes they get married, have families, and do just fine with Jesus. A mistake doesn't typically define or shape their ministry future unless it's gone unchecked for years and gotten progressively darker and damaging. It's easier for a man to conceal the truth and move on in life after he engages in sexual sin. Just look at the story of the woman caught in adultery in John chapter 8. There's no mention of the guy who was doing it with her. And things aren't much different today. It's more difficult for women to maintain the high regard of their religious community or continue to pursue a vocational ministry calling if they make a sexual mistake and get pregnant. Can you imagine being a single female in seminary or working in a church and getting pregnant outside of marriage? The stark reality is you'd be kicked out of school or get fired from your job. You'd essentially be disqualified from ministry—unlike your male colleagues who can probably "oops" and get away with it.

Don't risk making a sexual mistake that could result in an unplanned pregnancy. Let's get real for a moment. More often than not, everyone struggles with it. But as a Church, we've suffocated sexual sin behind a shroud of fear and shame to such a degree that it's uncommon for anyone to come up for air and be really honest about his or her struggles. Sexual brokenness continues in secrecy and can often get worse because no one is talking about it or dealing with it in helpful ways.

In paid or volunteer ministry, few get help or own up to their sexual struggles for fear of being dismissed, shunned, or fired. Honesty tends to result in dismissal not forgiveness. Hardly ever is a fresh start or new beginning offered to the sexually deviant. Maybe I'm exaggerating a bit (or a lot) to make a point, but I think I'd much rather recruit an honest and struggling volunteer or intern who's on the pill than someone who's living a double life and secretly having sex. Authenticity is much more spiritually mature and emotionally healthy than living a lie.

Honesty is what I'm really advocating for here. Have friends or mentors in your life with whom you can be real. People who will graciously help you stay accountable and steer you back on track if you do stumble. A youth pastor friend once told me that you know you have a true mentor when "you know so much about her that you can get her fired, and she knows so much about you that she can get you thrown in jail." That's the kind of honesty I'm talking about.

Women who feel forced to lie about their purity and sexual activity are typically the ones who are most at risk to end up pregnant. Women (and men) working in Christian organizations who are forced to sign behavioral contracts aren't given a safe space to be honest or address what is really going on in regard to sexual temptation or sexual identity struggles and questions. Young and single Christians oftentimes aren't self-aware enough of their own weaknesses to take the proper precautions to practice safe sex. When a person is forced to lie about sexual activity or orientation because of behavior contracts, no one benefits. Where is the opportunity for confession, forgiveness, and receiving helpful resources when needed? No one wants to lose a job or live with a damaged reputation due to an unplanned pregnancy.

Teri James, age 29, made headlines in 2013 after she filed a lawsuit against San Diego Christian College for firing her six months earlier because she had premarital sex and got pregnant.[33] The double standard here is that after Teri was fired, that same college offered her fiancé a job. A troubling double standard. Why should a woman who has sex before marriage be fired while a man who has sex before marriage gets hired? The whole thing is whacky.

*Impolite Company*, a snarky blog I love to read, points out:

> *If San Diego Christian College is determined to publish a strict set of moral behaviors and punish those who fail to live up to them, perhaps they should reconsider including the word* Christian *in their name. Or maybe they should spend a little more time reading the primary source material, where they'll find many, many, many passages like this:*
>
> > *Peter said to Jesus, "Lord, how many times should I forgive my brother or sister who sins against me? Should I forgive as many as seven times?"*
> >
> > *Jesus said, "Not just seven times, but rather as many as seventy-seven times."* (Matthew 18:21–22 CEB)
>
> *I know, I know, it's not nearly as fun to forgive people as it is to punish them.*[34]

Pregnancy makes a vulnerable and stressful time even more so when you're unmarried and working in a Christian-based organization or church. How many women—purely out of self-preservation—end up aborting their babies for fear of being found out and losing their jobs? Teri shares, "I was an unmarried, pregnant woman. And they took away my livelihood. They stripped me of my dignity and humiliated me. I not only lost my source of income and my health insurance to care for myself and my baby through my pregnancy, but I also lost my career and my community."[35] It's naïve to think young single women in ministry or those working for a Christian organization will never make a mistake. As we clearly see in this case, women are more at risk than men to lose their jobs, lose their healthcare, and be without help during a very exposed and emotional time.

The writer of the post on the *Impolite Company* blog shares, "I would not be surprised *at all* to learn that news of this story will lead other women who find themselves in Ms. James' situation to get an abortion because they can't afford to lose their job."[36]

Did you know that 13 percent of abortions (approximately 170,000 per year) are performed on self-described "born again" or evangelical Christians?[37] The percentage of Christian women having abortions hasn't dropped, even though the overall number of abortions has decreased in recent years. I know far too many female professors at Christian colleges, teachers at Christian schools, youth leaders, and volunteers who've been dismissed for getting pregnant outside of marriage. Yet, sexually active unmarried men often keep their jobs and have a much easier time hiding their sexual activity.

Married or not, make sure you have health insurance and a plan to protect yourself from a pregnancy you aren't ready for. Whether it's by courting and using chaperones à la Duggar style or having a safe place to own up to your own struggles, think about your sexual decisions and how they will impact your ministry opportunities.

When I was fresh out of college and beginning my first full-time paid youth ministry job, I found myself without birth control. I was a young, married, female youth director who had to go to Planned Parenthood or beg a doctor friend to write me a birth control prescription I couldn't afford to fill. So there I was—employed, uninsured, and sexually active in married bliss. You can imagine what happened next, right?

After I'd worked at this church for a year, the senior pastor called me into his office and told me how happy he was that my husband and I didn't have kids yet (so I could focus solely on my job). He wanted me to come up with a game plan to hit some big numerical benchmarks that year (*The Prayer of Jabez* was big at that time[38]) and not be distracted by having babies. That was sure a lot to accomplish with no health insurance. He said this to me right after I'd taken a drink of water, and I nearly spit it out of my mouth in shock. And then the pregnancy hormones kicked in. (I was five weeks pregnant at the time.) So I did what all pregnant women do when they're stressed, surprised, and feeling overwhelmed...I cried! That was awkward. Try back-pedaling out of that remark, dear senior pastor, while a pregnant lady sobs in your office.

I became a mom at age 23. My husband and I were one of those "get married too young because you want to have sex" kind of Christian college couples. Not that I regret it. But I'm pretty sure that if we'd had easy access to birth control, we would have waited longer to start a family so I could focus more on my career. Nevertheless, I come from a long line of Hispanic women who had children before the age of 19. In my family I'm a first-generation college graduate. I was also the first in my mother's immediate family to be born in the United States. So to be an American citizen, out of my teens, married, and with a college degree was already a huge accomplishment in their eyes. Kind of a big deal.

Obviously, a lack of health insurance and no access to birth control didn't help me thrive in my career or hit any huge benchmarks in my youth ministry before I had kids. So instead of focusing on my career and making my numbers-focused senior pastor happy, I thought about cutting back at work so I could focus on this baby who was about to enter the world. There was no one to coach me on how to manage both a baby and my ministry—especially not in my male-dominated, workaholic, numbers-focused work environment.

So my advice to you is to figure out how to get or ask for health insurance. The reality of married and unmarried women who can't afford to have children and are forced to give up a job, secretly terminate a pregnancy, or abandon their call to ministry makes birth control so important. Don't allow yourself to be in a position where you're forced to end your career or give up your calling just because you're uninsured and without dependable contraception. There are so many women, like myself, who end up begging doctor friends or visiting Planned Parenthood clinics for birth control because a church or Christian organization won't provide what they need.

I love what Rachel Held Evans wrote in her blog post "Privilege and The Pill": "Let's avoid making generalizations about the millions of women and families who say they would benefit from affordable, accessible contraception."[39] Maybe there are other first-generation college grads who want to enjoy married life and get established in a career before they have kids. Maybe, like myself, they need access to birth control so they can accomplish what their immigrant mothers and grandmothers could not. With access to affordable contraception, new dreams can come to fruition. New stories can be written. My mom had me when she was 18. My grandmother had my mom when she was 18. I wanted to chart a new path for myself.

If I haven't made it clear yet, let me spell it out for you one more time: Whether you're a volunteer youth worker or a paid one, protect your ministry by protecting yourself sexually. Maybe you do that by waiting to kiss until your wedding day, courting, or finding a mentor couple with whom you can be real and honest about your struggles. Just make sure you have a safe place to own up to your own imperfections and struggles with someone who isn't going to shame or fire you.

## PRESBYS

After my son was born, I left that SBC church for a position at a Presbyterian church in the North County Inland region of San Diego. It was a church with an egalitarian view of women in ministry, which was awesome. I worked there for eight years, and I enjoyed fair pay, a retirement plan, health insurance, access to affordable contraception, and other benefits. The funny thing is, back when I was young and fresh out of a Baptist Bible college, I told myself, *I'd never want to live in North County Inland* (it's too far from the beach and from my extended family). I also said, *I'd never want to work at a Presbyterian church.*

You can probably guess what happened. The church I didn't want to like ended up being the one I loved. I clicked with the people and found a wonderful place to do youth ministry. Even though I wasn't a Presbyterian, I learned a lot about leadership, vision, fair pay, and what it looked like to work in a place where women can serve in a leadership capacity. I got to experience time in the pulpit and get a feel for what egalitarian theology had to offer me. Being treated as an equal in ministry without gender limitations prompted me to wrestle with the limitations of my own theology.

I discovered I can preach thanks to Presby Bob and Rev. Jim who gave me opportunities to assist regularly in worship and invited me to preach a couple of times a year. Not only was

I allowed to preach, but I was really good at it too. Older women, middle-aged adults, and teens met me by the door after each sermon, affirming me with handshakes, high-fives, and genuine compliments. It was always a fun surprise to hear how many CDs of my teachings the congregants had requested (podcasting was a new thing at that time), and it further validated my teaching gifts as well. This preaching thing was something I was good at. As the pastors on staff modeled healthy leadership to me and helped me grow as a woman in youth ministry, I was forced to rethink the limitations that my complementarian theology had placed on me.

But even in a church with an egalitarian view of women in leadership, there were still challenges. Old men would shake my hand and comment on the length of my skirt, or old women might comment negatively about my shoes or let me know whether or not I should be wearing socks. One time the dad of a youth group student reached out and stroked my hair while he was talking to me in the hallway. Seminary didn't teach me how to handle unwanted physical attention from men. I had to figure out how to kindly but firmly establish boundaries and personal space. I learned a lot during my years with the PCUSA, and at a church that wasn't even on my radar.

I wouldn't have had any of the youth ministry positions I've landed without being willing to move or try something outside of my own theological framework. Like any job or new ministry venture, you have to knock on a lot of doors and sometimes step out in faith, trusting that it's going to be a good long-term match. If you're willing to move, try a different church or take on a paid or volunteer position that's a bit outside your comfort zone. You just might find a match made in heaven. Working with the Presbyterians opened the door to where I find myself today, and it taught me some lifelong lessons.

# PAYCHECKS

When you think about great jobs, you often think about good pay. It's only natural. So I often get asked about compensation for women in youth ministry. Just last week my good friend told me about a private Christian school in the Bible Belt that asks female staff to sign a document saying *they're okay getting paid less than the male teachers*. The justification for this decision is that men are the providers for their families, and thus they should get paid more. The women, on the other hand, are expected to have husbands who provide for them. I've heard similar stories from women in youth ministry. Wow. That logic makes me crazy!

Women in youth ministry often ask me, "How do I know if I'm being paid fairly or being taken for a ride?" Unfortunately, most youth workers (regardless of gender) get paid way less than they should be. It's also true that because of our gender, a lot of women in youth ministry get paid much less *and* they don't get the opportunities that many men in our field do. As a result, women push themselves harder to achieve because they have to. Many job opportunities in youth ministry are intended for men, not women. Most camps, conferences, and retreats will hire guys as speakers but not us gals. I've heard it over and over again: "Sorry, we're looking for God's *man* for the job."

The idea of fair pay went through my mind as I was sitting on a church bus a few summers back. We were driving two big school buses to summer camp. Eighty students came with us—60 girls and 20 boys. I started thinking back to our Six Flags Magic Mountain trip in the fall. Two busloads of kids again: 80 percent of the students on the trip were female. I thought about it a little longer. The male youth pastor, with a really small percentage of male students in the youth ministry, was getting paid twice as much as I was. Both of us received a pastoral housing allowance. It was Southern California…with a high cost of living and slightly larger paychecks.

Do the math. This doesn't seem very "complementary" to me when both jobs (his and mine) were essentially the same. Same seminary education, same years of experience, and only one year difference in tenure. It was time to rethink my theology of women in ministry. Time to rethink a lot of things—especially if I wanted to survive in Southern California with a high cost of living.

## BECAUSE I'M WORTH IT
### BY RACHEL BLOM

I never chose youth ministry; it chose me. And to make it even worse (or better, depending on your perspective): I had fully expected it to choose my husband.

You see, we started in youth ministry together, my husband and me. And we were both good at it, although in different ways. He's a leader, a visionary, and an excellent coach who can inspire people to do better. I'm a leader too, but more the manager type. Plus, I'm a born teacher and an evangelist. Still, I always thought God would choose my husband to be the youth pastor, considering he was a man and all that. Well, God didn't. He chose me.

When the church we were volunteering in needed a (volunteer) youth ministry coordinator, my husband did it for one year and then handed the job over to me, with great relief. He hated it. I loved it. But at the time I also had a job as a manager in a hospital. Soon, the two jobs became harder and harder to combine. I reduced my hours, changed jobs, and managed to combine 24 hours a week in the hospital with about the same number of volunteer hours in youth ministry.

Then I became pregnant. It was very much planned and very much wanted, but it created a huge problem. There was no way I could work two 24-hour jobs and also be a mom. So I told the church to either put me on the payroll or I'd quit the youth ministry.

That's when I made a huge mistake. I wanted that job so bad, I wanted to work in the church so much, and the elders knew it. So when they offered me the job at a ridiculously low salary, I accepted. My husband worked full time and we figured we could make it work—even with the extra expenses for the baby.

And we did make it work. But the two years I worked at that church cost us all of our savings. When we eventually left that church (because my husband got a job 500 miles away), we had no savings left—nothing.

At first, I was okay with the meager income. Youth ministry is a calling, right? And obeying a calling means making sacrifices. Plus, our money belonged to God anyway, so it was His to do with as He pleased. Or so I reasoned. My husband wasn't as convinced as I was about the fairness of it all, but he accepted it because he knew how much I wanted that job.

At some point the church decided to hire another staff member, a small groups and pastoral care coordinator. The person they hired was a young man I knew well because he'd interned in my youth ministry. He was 10 years younger than me, he had no work experience, and he was coming to this job straight out of Bible college. I was excited for him that he got the job.

Then I accidently learned what they'd offered him for a salary—it was substantially more than what they'd offered me. When I asked the elders about it, they explained it was because he was "the breadwinner of the family." He needed the salary because his wife was pregnant and couldn't work full time after the baby arrived.

I was so hurt, so disappointed, and so angry. How could they do this? How could they rationalize paying him more than they did me? I'd never realized that the fact that I am a woman had factored into my low salary. I'd never even considered that my gender would play a role in my perceived "worth." But apparently it did.

It took me a long time to let go of this anger and get a proper perspective on the situation. Primarily, the mistake was mine. I should have never accepted that salary in the first place. My husband had been right: I'd wanted the job too much to be reasonable about it.

I chose not to make a fuss about it since I was leaving anyway, and the church was already in a crisis due to two pastors being at odds with each other. I could have sued the church, and I probably would have won—but at what cost? I decided to let it go and I've never regretted it. I still visit this church and even preach there a few times a year, and it's okay. I truly love that church, even if they did treat me badly.

But I learned at least one valuable thing through that experience: my worth. Never again will I consent to being treated less than because I'm a woman. I deserve equal pay because I'm worth it.

Women who want and need equal pay for equal work are often ambitious, working harder to prove themselves. And they must do this to make ends meet and compete for positions that typically get filled by men. Some women will occasionally upstage the guys they work with or work for. I've seen my share of guys squirm when this happens. When we get speaking gigs or cool things happen in our careers, I've seen (and heard about this happening from several other women in youth ministry) the men we work with or hang out with get weird.

Women have a difficult time being successful. A good friend of mine who works for a parachurch ministry began to get noticed by the national office. She was asked to participate in national trainings and was paid to travel and speak about what she was doing with other chapters of her organization. As her ministry thrived, her male supervisor, who'd been working for the same organization much longer than she had, grew more insecure. She was advancing and he wasn't. Things got tense. He became more and more critical of her work, and their work relationship became toxic. Board members eventually got involved, and several meetings were held to address the situation. In the end the board stood by her, but a 15-year ministry friendship between her and her supervisor ended. Why does this happen so often?

Many men don't realize how much harder women have to work in order to perform and prove ourselves as "high capacity candidates" with amazing teaching skills. If we don't, then we don't stand a chance at landing the jobs, promotions, and speaking invitations that come so easily to them. This isn't true in every context, but it's true more often than not. Sheryl Sandberg writes in *Lean In*, "When a man is successful, he is liked by both men and women. When a woman is successful, people of both genders like her less."[40] This is sadly true, and I've seen it happen too often.

Even when women in ministry are successful, they still aren't given the same pay and benefits as men. How do you know if you're getting paid fairly? Perhaps you want to pay (all of) your bills, and you dream of being able to afford a real vacation someday. Getting paid fairly would sure help with that, huh? My general rule of thumb is to find out what teachers are earning in your area. Your job is in many ways similar to a schoolteacher's, although your summers and breaks are usually much busier (with camps and mission trips). Look at your education and years of experience, and then compare your pay schedule to a teacher's. Keep in mind that schoolteachers also get retirement and medical benefits.

What should your salary be based on the teachers in your area? If you're getting paid *way less* than what a teacher makes (like not even step 1), then you might be grossly underpaid. This is especially true if you have a degree and completed a ministry internship (equivalent to student teaching). If you're supervising multiple staff, considered responsible for the well-being of hundreds of families, and required to hit huge benchmarks (think department head in a large church equals the vice principal of a school), then you should be paid accordingly. Look online for a website to help you compare one area to another before you get too crazy about the numbers.

Another helpful tool for figuring out fair compensation is to take a look at the salaries of larger denominations. If you're good with your Googling skills, you can find published pay scales on the Internet from school districts and mainline denomination churches in your area. If you want a more depressing view of youth pastor pay, look at *Group Magazine's The 2012 Youth Ministry Salary Survey*.[41] They publish one of these reports every two years. It will give you a realistic (and kind of sad) look at what youth pastors actually get paid across the United States.

Group's salary survey makes it clear that there is a huge discrepancy between what male and female youth workers get paid. On average, women get paid $27,000 annually, and men get paid $41,200 annually. What isn't clear is whether these numbers are for full-time or part-time positions. So I asked. Here's what Rick Lawrence, the editor of *Group Magazine* and the author of the 2012 salary survey, had to say:

> *All of the figures on the salary survey reflect full-time, paid positions. There has always been a significant disparity in salaries between men and women in youth ministry. In some cases, it reflects the longevity of male youth workers in paid positions versus women—more men have been paid for youth ministry for a longer time than women. That means their longevity has translated to getting paid higher on the continuum. But some of it is simple gender inequity—churches have tended to pay men in ministry positions more than women doing the same job.*

Full time or part time, it's hard to argue that there isn't a pay problem here. I spent some time during the summer of 2013 assisting a church that had taken a full-time position, previously held by a male youth pastor (paid around $50K), and split it into two part-time positions (paid $25K each). The church had a difficult time filling these part-time positions with experienced male youth workers because men were often the ones who needed full-time jobs to support their families. So they hired two women instead.

This particular church has an abundance of part-time paid women on staff. A lot of women want to work fewer hours so they can be home more with their children. And women are more willing to accept a lower-paid part-time position as a trade-off for the schedule flexibility they need. It seems like a win-win situation—or is it? In all honesty, the women often worked more hours than they were paid for. Even so, they enjoyed the flexibility their "part-time" positions gave them to chaperone their children's field trips or work from home more easily. No one was complaining.

If you're in a similar situation, it's a good idea to compare your pay to what a part-time or substitute teacher makes in your area and see if a part-time gig is worth it—especially since nothing is ever really "part time" in ministry.

Men and women deserve to receive equal pay that's not influenced or changed by their marital status or having a family. A person's pay needs to be objective, which is why I love a pay scale based only on experience, skill, longevity, and the demands of the position. It's not right to pay women less when they're doing the same job as men. And according to his 2014 State of the Union address, President Obama agrees with me:

> Today, women make up about half our workforce. But they still make 77 cents for every dollar a man earns. That is wrong, and in 2014, it's an embarrassment. A woman deserves equal pay for equal work. She deserves to have a baby without sacrificing her job. A mother deserves a day off to care for a sick child or sick parent without running into hardship—and you know what, a father does, too. It's time to do away with workplace policies that belong in a "Mad Men" episode. This year, let's all come together—Congress, the White House, and businesses from Wall Street to

*Main Street—to give every woman the opportunity she deserves. Because I firmly believe when women succeed, America succeeds.*[42]

I know no one chooses to go into ministry for the money (duh!), and fewer churches today are hiring paid youth workers. Yet there are still vocational youth workers who have families to take care of. It's not selfish to dream of being able to send your kids to college someday or pay for their braces. And I sure don't want to see hoards of retired youth workers living on the street or working at Walmart in their old age because they have zero money saved for retirement. If a church wants to hire a professional, they need to offer professional-level compensation. Churches often get what they pay for.

# QUESTIONS FOR REFLECTION

1. Health insurance and the pill—what are your thoughts on how they help or hinder women in ministry?

2. If you're in a paid youth ministry position, are you receiving the same compensation and insurance benefits as the male pastors on staff? Why or why not?

3. Should sexual sin disqualify someone from an internship or from leading in youth ministry? Why or why not? What if they're honest about their struggles and getting the support and accountability they need to make better choices?

4. Read John 8:2-11. How did Jesus treat the woman caught in adultery? How did the religious community treat her? How did they treat the man who was with her?

5. What do you think about behavior contracts? Do they negatively impact the authenticity of those who truly want to follow Jesus? Do you think a lot of pastors and ministry volunteers stumble alone in hidden sin for fear of being dismissed or fired?

6. Do you think churches treat sexual sin differently than other types of sin? Why or why not?

7. Would you accept lower pay if it meant a more flexible schedule to be with your kids or to work from home?

8. How have you handled unwanted attention from men as a female youth worker? Has anyone ever commented on the way you dress? How do you handle awkward situations that may come up as you lead in youth ministry?

9. What did you agree with in this chapter? What challenged you? What did you disagree with?

# 11

# BOYCOTTED FOR BEING A GIRL (PASTOR)

I spent a little bit of time in between youth ministry jobs helping out as a high school pastor. It was super fun, but it was also challenging. I was filling in for a really great, personable man who'd left to take a job at a larger church in town. If you are new to a youth ministry position, particularly if you're working a new gig at a church with a youth pastor–centered model of ministry, there will be challenges as you try to fill someone else's rather large shoes. It's tough to follow a high-energy, personable youth pastor whose "charm" or charisma turns out to be the primary sustaining force of the youth ministry. It's a difficult youth ministry model to sustain long term.

Even though I was going to be there for only a short time, a handful of well-meaning youth group kids drove home the point that, in their minds, it would have been better if the church had hired *a man* for the job. Someone who can grow facial hair and rock a cool beard. (In other words, *not* me.) After being left without a youth pastor because their beloved, enormously tall, bald, and charismatic *male* youth leader had left them for a new position elsewhere, these students did not want a 5' 0", female, and much less charming *me* leading them. They weren't shy about voicing their opposition either. While I was visiting the youth group on a Wednesday night, one observant teen said to me, "You are like the *exact opposite* of our last youth pastor." Yes, it was true. Well, except for the fact that we've both spent years loving Jesus and teenagers, and doing youth ministry.

I was not the guy they were looking for. Honestly, I don't think they would have been happy with anyone at that point—not even a guy. They missed their youth leader, and adolescents want what they know. They wanted a replica of their former youth pastor.

My first Sunday on the job as their new *female* youth pastor was interesting. Several teens staged a boycott and chose not to attend youth group or partake in the welcome breakfast that was held in my honor between worship services. Thankfully, it was a problem that longevity fixes. Eventually you become the norm, and memories of former youth pastors fade into the background. Being boycotted for being a girl kinda sucked, but I sipped my coffee and reminded myself that it was their hurt speaking. Immature, irrational teens were still reeling from the aftershocks of change.

What made a sucky situation even worse was that two weeks into my brief time there, the chief protester who'd been circling the wagons against me suddenly and unexpectedly passed away. He'd been dating another student in the youth group who also wasn't about to give me the time of day. She was now facing a tremendously painful loss, and I was probably the last person she wanted to talk to. Now you have a bunch of hurting kids who are thrust deep into crisis mode with an outsider as their youth pastor. Welcome to youth ministry. When students are hurting, they want what's familiar, what's comfortable. In this case, they wanted their former tall, bald, male youth pastor who came to save the day. I was totally fine with it. I mean, who wants a stranger around in crisis?

Knowing that longevity eventually wins out and I could

someday become the "new normal" is a great way to work through such obvious gender bias, but is that really the goal? So, yes, someday I could have been "the familiar." After spending a week bonding with them at summer camp, several of them apologized for giving me such a hard time. We made a ton of progress. Unfortunately, I wasn't going to be their interim youth pastor for too much longer. I could have become what they're used to...their beloved female youth pastor. But I want something better than that.

I want to see a youth ministry centered on connecting teenagers into the church body, not enabling an overdependence on one youth pastor. It's so much healthier for teens to be connected to several adults in the church and not dependent on the personality, charisma, age, or gender of the youth pastor on stage. For a great book about the integration of youth into the church, as opposed to a disconnected youth pastor-centered student ministry, check out *Redefining the Role of the Youth Worker* by April L. Diaz.[43]

Teens who are used to having a male youth pastor might not be the only ones who have trouble with the whole female youth pastor thing. One day I saw on Facebook that a group of pastors' wives from my church were getting together once a month to assemble meals for their freezer.

Now, I must confess that I have a weird love for meal planning. I don't know why because we don't eat that many home-cooked meals. But as a little girl, I loved shopping with my mom for groceries, and I'd make imaginary meal plans in my head. My fascination with championing the priority of the family dinner hour as a ministry has led me to teach fun little workshops to women's groups like MOPS (Mothers of Preschoolers).[44]

But back to the pastors' wives...I'd hung out with these women. I'd gone to their homes and watched *Twilight* and

*The Hunger Games.* So I was super excited they were doing something that I'm a pro at doing (making freezer meals). I sent one of them a Facebook message that said something like, "Hey, I saw you ladies are making freezer meals together. I'd love to make meals with you sometime." I wasn't selling them anything, I wasn't trying to take over their group, I just thought it would be fun to join them. I got no response. *Not a word.* I later found out that this was a "pastors' wives only" get together, and since I'm not a pastor's wife, I was not invited. Boycotted for being a girl pastor.

Since I wasn't a male pastor, I didn't get invited to the males-only pastoral get-togethers either. I wasn't a young college intern, so I rarely got invited to their gigs—unless it was a mentoring thing, a family event, or I was buying. I am self-aware enough to know that I'm not socially awkward or lame to hang out with…people like me and I do have friends. I just live in this weird space of being a female youth pastor, and sometimes people don't know what social space to invite me into.

Sometimes we women in youth ministry feel unfairly boycotted when, in truth, the distance we sense between others and ourselves is just unfamiliarity. We have to extend the invitation, be the inviters, and initiate the relationships sometimes. Draw people in and help them get more and more comfortable with female pastors instead of caving in to their bias or feeling disgruntled and resentful of their initial coldness toward you.

Women who work in environments with a hierarchical or complementarian view of women in ministry might also feel boycotted because of their gender. It's possible you'll miss out on job promotions and have your giftedness handicapped by the "acceptable," gender-determined, separate-but-equal roles for ministry. These are the types of churches where women are often limited to doing "girls ministry" or asked to oversee curriculum and the organization of small groups—the things "girls can do." There will likely be pastoral or teaching roles you won't be allowed to fill. If that way of doing things matches your theology, great. But if not, then make sure you work and serve in a place that does.

## SHOULD I STAY OR SHOULD I GO?
### BY MORGAN SCHMIDT

My first name, Morgan, can go either way—male or female. So there's nothing like the deafening silence I hear on the other end of the line when a pastor or a church's search committee calls me for an interview and realizes I'm a woman. "It's not Mr. Morgan—it's actually *Mrs.* Morgan." Please, people. If you're dead set on having a godly young man be your new youth pastor, then express that clearly in your job description so I don't waste my time dreaming of how I can love and serve your teenagers and their families. There was a time when I was constantly reminding myself that if the church didn't want me just because I'm a woman, then there's no way I wanted to be a part of their community.

I get torn sometimes, thinking maybe I should take one for the team and infiltrate one of these bastions of male superiority. I could heroically change the theology and culture from the inside out. Many women have stayed and fought and sacrificed in order to gain access and influence for women like me, and I'm incredibly grateful to walk in their legacy. Maybe that will be *my* role somewhere, at some point. But sometimes the most revolutionary thing we can do is insist on being who we are and finding communities of faith that will support us. Trust me, churches would begin to notice, change, or die if all the women who were gifted for ministry insisted on serving in a place where they're wanted and empowered.

It took me a few church positions to learn how to honor myself as a woman in ministry. I realized that direct, honest communication was really important to me, and passive aggression is death to me. Ignoring my emotional responses because they make my male colleagues uncomfortable is to deny one of the best gifts God has given me. I care more about the aesthetic in the youth room than messy games. And all of that is not only okay, but good.

If you're in a place that is sucking the life out of you, forcing you to participate in masculine structures of power and authority that crush your spirit, then maybe it's time to go. I don't say that lightly. Pursuing life can be so costly. But we follow in the way of a God who says we're worth it.

Really, the point isn't to be a woman in youth ministry. The point is to be me, and I'm a woman. The more that I live into and pastor out of my whole, feminine self, the better I'll be able to help students live into their authentic selves.

Theologically driven limitations of women in pastoral ministry can breed conflict when an abusive or struggling male leader is in charge of gifted female staff. If someone is leading from a place of emotional and spiritual health, there will be an atmosphere of empowerment, respect, and good communication. Healthy leadership minimizes gender bias and feelings of low self-worth, and it also reduces conflict.

The painful time when I had to deal with a lot of ongoing mismanagement issues between a former male colleague and myself (see chapter 6) eventually led to some difficult conversations. Bad leadership, poor management, terrible communication, and other things had all contributed to a disastrous work environment. There was a long trail of dismissed and unhappy interns and volunteers—most of them female. Fear of confrontation and an apprehension about possibly getting a bad reference for the next job interview kept everyone silent. Rarely did anyone speak up. So unhealthy continues to breed unhealthy, and nothing ever gets better.

I finally spoke up and defined my own boundaries. After an executive pastor took the time to hear me out, I knew two things to be true: (1) I was right, and (2) It wouldn't change anything because I'm a girl. I remember sitting on a brown leather sofa in his office when he looked at me and said, "Well, we can't have a woman lead this ministry," as though for a brief moment he'd entertained the idea of firing the guy and keeping me on staff, which wasn't what I wanted either. He simply shook his head and said, "No, no, we can't do that."

I now knew for certain that I'd never have an equal voice in this ministry setting. Never. The theology of where I was working no longer matched my own. I didn't want my pastoral calling to be limited by my gender, nor was a patriarchal work environment healthy to my soul. As you can probably guess, I didn't stay there much longer after that. I was done having my gifts limited and my voice silenced because I was a girl.

# QUESTIONS FOR REFLECTION

1. Have you ever been boycotted for being a girl in ministry?

2. How is a pastor- or personality-centered model of youth ministry difficult to sustain?

3. Have there been times when you've been left out of something because you weren't a pastor's wife or a male pastor on staff? What happened? How did you feel about that?

4. How does longevity win over the turbulent tide of unwanted change?

5. What do you do about uncomfortable mismanagement issues that never get addressed?

6. How does your church integrate youth into the larger church community? Are your teens connected to other adults in the congregation beyond the walls of the youth room?

7. What do you love about this chapter? What are you having a hard time with? What's challenging you?

# 12

# THE MARRIED YOUTH WORKER

After 16 years of marriage, I can say with 100 percent certainty that I really love my husband. I also finally figured out why my house isn't always company ready. My dishes aren't always done. My sink isn't always shining. It's largely due to our "no work after 8 p.m." rule. When the kids are finally in bed, the lunches are packed, and the coffee pot is prepped with the Mr. Coffee Fresh Brew™ Timer set for a 6:30 a.m. wake-up call, we call it a night in our house. Unless company is coming, a forgotten field trip needs a last-minute sack lunch, or some major project is due in the morning, *we are fine leaving some chores undone.* We don't squeeze in enough date nights (baby-sitters are expensive!), so we *love* 8 p.m. We *live* for 8 p.m. It's our time to pour a big glass of Diet Coke (or wine, if you're allowed), sink into the sofa, and snuggle up with Netflix or Hulu Plus.

Do you know why my husband and I still like each other? Because we don't clean the carpet, fold laundry, or tackle any household chores *after 8 p.m.* Instead, we hang out. If there's a project to be done, we leave it for spring break, Christmas break, a Saturday afternoon, or summer vacation. The beauty of being married to a teacher...there is always a school break around every corner. I realize not everyone can be married to a teacher. But for all you single youth workers out there: I highly recommend it! His teaching schedule is what makes the craziness of my ministry schedule work.

My husband loves the 8 p.m. rule. After a long day of work, we both have our fair share of early evening responsibilities. I make dinner; he cleans up. I give the girls baths and comb their tangled hair. He empties the trash. I make sure kids put on their PJs and brush their teeth. He makes sandwiches for the next day's lunches. I put the kids to bed and do devos with them (or at least *think* about doing devos with them...let's be honest here). He runs the dishwasher, walks the dog, and does a quick living room pick-up. He looks forward to 8 p.m. like a mini vacation. He loves it when nothing else is being asked of him. He needs to recharge his batteries with downtime too. Especially as a teacher who's been surrounded by kids *all day long*, downtime is essential to keeping him a happy camper.

With a familiar predictability each evening (whenever we're at home, anyway), he asks me, "So, what do you want to watch tonight?" Or he plops down two Netflix envelopes and excitedly tells me about my movie choices. He loves getting the mail. There's something fun about opening up the mailbox and finding Netflix movies in a cool red envelope. Yes, my husband regularly needs some downtime from 8 p.m. to 11 p.m., or else we hate each other come Saturday morning.

Our premarital counseling taught us one important thing that we both remember well, even all these years later: We are 100 percent compatible in one particular area. Can you guess which one? Entertainment. Our mentor's jaw dropped and he said, "No couple is ever 100 percent compatible in *any* area, but you guys scored 100 percent in entertainment! That never happens!" That's why the 8 p.m. (or sometimes 8:30 p.m.) rule is vital for us. We connect best through downtime—through fun! Anyone who knows us knows one thing for sure: We are *fun*! Something we've known since our very first date is that we sure know how to enjoy life together. And our 8 p.m. rule gives us space to do just that. We might need to hire a housekeeper, though.

## TO MULTITASK OR *NOT* TO MULTITASK?

The 8 p.m. rule is great for silencing the call to unload the dishwasher or for ignoring the buzzer signaling it's time to take a load of clothes out of the dryer. But what about the beckoning call of the Siren that is my MacBook? Or the enticing iPad within arm's reach? During downtime, I can (too) easily make my way over to my Sunday sermon on Google Drive for a quick update or tweak. And I love browsing Twitter and YouTube for relevant content to use in a lesson. The temptation to multitask during downtime is alluring. So I give in. A lot.

I multitask while chilling out because it gives me a chance to catch up or get ahead with the admin side of ministry. It's also fun. While I *love* the "being in the trenches with people" aspect of face-to-face ministry time, I also enjoy the behind-the-scenes admin side of it. I find joy in creating, designing, dreaming, and prepping a relevant message for Sunday morning that I can't wait to deliver. Because I like ministry, I give no second thought to multitasking, or should I say "working," during the evenings while I hit the pause button on everything else (including household chores and the care and feeding of my husband). That can be a problem because I need to model for my own children and the teens in my youth ministry that my husband is a priority. My ministry at home is just as important as the one at church.

Multitasking begins to take a toll in that moment when I'm watching a TV show or a movie and I suddenly have no idea what's happening. When my husband is nearby but we're sitting on opposite sides of the sofa, I can get too immersed in what I'm doing to move over and lean against his warm shoulder. So if the movie or TV program is *really* good, it wins

what my husband calls the "She Closed Her Laptop Award."
He smiles and feels a sense of victory in picking a movie or TV
program that I liked so much. It's a win. When it's engaging,
when I am captivated and invested in the story, everything else
stops. I put away the electronics, lean in a bit, sit closer to my
husband, and I am completely engaged. In those moments I
realize that ministry has taken over and I need to turn it off and
make my husband a higher priority.

On those days when I have a migraine from looking at a screen
too long, or when I've logged way too many hours at work,
or when my mind is racing a million miles a minute, I stop. I
enjoy the evening. I enjoy my husband. I leave my phone in the
car so it's easier to ignore. A healthy marriage requires space
with no work demands lingering in the background. It feels
good to stop! I need to do this way more often. Sometimes an
escape to a backyard hot tub, a swimming pool, or even the
bathtub is in order (because electronics and bubble baths are
not a good combo). When the temptation to work instead of
recharge keeps recurring in your life...grab your spouse and get
into a space that requires all electronics be put away. *Turn off
everything.*

You two need time to reconnect, relax, and enjoy your marriage
during the workweek. Otherwise, you'll be tired and grumpy
with each other all week, and then you'll wonder why you're
short-tempered and annoyed with each other every Saturday
morning. If you aren't intentional about creating space during
the workweek to have fun with your honey, it will set a bad
vibe once the weekend finally arrives.

## HIS CAREER OR HERS?

My amazing husband supported my call to ministry and my
career by giving up his job for mine. It was a huge decision.
It was a difficult decision to move from San Diego to Grand
Rapids for a job. In San Diego my husband taught at a school

he loved and that loved him right back. And to make matters worse, my husband's brother had just gotten a job at that school, and he moved from Orange County to San Diego to teach there. My husband was so excited to have his brother on the faculty at his school and living so close to us. So, yeah, his dream of working with his brother got sidelined because of me.

It was a big change for us; but as we said yes to God, we said yes to moving forward in faith. Sometimes I can't stop feeling unworthy of the sacrifice he made so I could pursue my dream. Yet here we are…willing to move where God leads and begin a new adventure. Ultimately, a huge move that requires one spouse to give up his or her job for the other's has to be more about what God wants and less about what the two of you want. It can't be about "her career" or "his career." Big changes like a cross-country move impact your entire family and launch everyone into a whole new trajectory. My kids' friends have changed. *My* friends have changed. The frequency of visits with extended family has changed. Our church home has changed.

Don't make it a fight, a gender war, or a power struggle. Instead, pray together and seek where God is leading your family. When it's right, you will look at each other and say, "This is home." Just like we did when we visited Grand Rapids. Plus, what makes a better story? The one where you stayed comfortable? Or the one where you both took a risk and said yes to something big and maybe even a little bit scary?

But what if you work at two different churches?

I've noticed that married couples who work at or attend two different churches are a lot more common than my conservative evangelical background led me to believe. After hanging out with mainliners (Presbyterians, Nazarenes, and Methodists) more often, I've seen *many* ministry couples who work at two different churches. To them, it's a no-brainer and a nonissue. But to a lot of us who grew up in conservative Protestant churches with more traditional gender roles, we still struggle with this idea.

I asked a friend and former youth intern of mine, Mariah Sherman, to share her experience with you. When the husband and wife work at two different churches and the wife also works in a pastoral role, it could be a tricky situation for any couple. But that's especially true when a conservative church with a strong complementarian theology employs the husband. Here is Mariah's story:

> *"I am so excited for you!" I said to my husband. And I really was. After years of paying his dues, my husband had finally gotten his dream job at a fantastic church. The only trouble was, I'd just landed my dream job at a different yet also fantastic church. Now what?*

> *As word got around that we were working at different churches, we started getting funny looks. Heck, even my non-Christian friends thought it was a bit weird. "So, you're working for the competition?" (That's a different topic for another time!)*

> *Riddled with guilt, I assumed it must be my duty, as the wife, to quit my job. So I put in my notice. As I finished up my time at my fantastic church, neither my husband nor I felt great about my decision. Weren't we supposed to feel better? After all, everyone had been telling us this is what God wanted us to do!*

> *Later that month, a few positions at my former church got rearranged, and what do you know—I was working for them again. And I got a promotion. Oops! It looks like we're going to be working at two different churches for a while.*

*Still, we feel the church family is immensely important, so we were concerned about being separated. We both wanted to make sure we didn't miss out on this important aspect of our spouse's life. So here's what we did:*

- *My husband's church has a great Sunday evening service that I attend each week. It's terrific to see all the amazing work this church is doing!*
- *My husband attends youth group with me on Wednesday nights. The teens* love *him, and I love that our teenagers get to see a married couple serving God.*
- *Last year, we joined a coed small group at my church. This year, we're part of a coed small group at my husband's church.*
- *We try our best to avoid using the terms "his church" or "her church"; instead, we remind ourselves that we're both working for God's church.*

*While small, these tweaks to how we approach our church lives have brought a lot of joy into our marriage and our ministries. Perhaps God has us working in two different locations during this season of our life (or perhaps forever?), but that doesn't change how unified we are in our calling to serve God in our community. It is for this purpose that God has brought us together, and in this purpose our marriage will stand.*

## RULES FOR A HAPPY MARRIAGE AS A YOUTH WORKER

My husband and I put together a list of what has worked for us over the years…

**1. Create a rhythm to your week.** Carve out time to connect with your spouse and figure out a time period that you will jealously guard as "yours," without iPhone notifications or ministry demands beckoning to you every five minutes.

This is a time to stay physically, emotionally, and spiritually connected. If your ministry and coworkers always get your best and all that's left over for your husband is a tired, stressed-out, and emotional mess, then something has to change.

**2. Don't be afraid to leave some things undone.** If you're tired and your spouse is worn out and grumpy because there is no downtime between work, kids, and household chores, you need to change something. If you run ragged Monday through Friday and expect a weekend to help you recharge and make up for a hellish week, it's not going to be enough. If going to bed with dirty dishes in the sink means an extra chunk of time to enjoy and have sex with your spouse, than leave those dishes in the sink.

**3. Schedule no more than two work nights a week.** Plan your schedule and any evening meetings so you're gone from home no more than two nights a week. This is especially important if your spouse has a traditional work schedule with only evenings and weekends at home. If you break this rule, make it up to your spouse by adding some hours somewhere else in your schedule when you will be home or can sneak away for a midday lunch date.

**4. Give your spouse a say in your youth event calendar.** When we lived in Southern California, every year, I blocked out the dates for the San Diego Comic Con. I'd do whatever it took to have time off that week so he could do his thing and attend Comic Con with his friends. I didn't plan a mission trip or summer camp for that week—ever. My ministry calendar can't always and forever trump his calendar. Christmas and Easter are busy times for ministry staff, but my church obligations can't always mess up the holidays for him. If my ministry schedule creates a lack of family togetherness and keeps us away from his brothers and family each year, I have to be proactive and take some holidays off or get creative and find ways to share holiday responsibilities with my coworkers. And even in Michigan, it's still a non-negotiable for Tim to do his Comic Con thing.

**5. Get Disneyland passes (or something like them).** One thing that works well for us is some kind of escape. We need a place where we can get away and out of the house together. A place where cell phones don't work. A place where you're not going to think about bills, laundry, your blog, Twitter, or your Sunday lesson. A place away from it all where your headspace is completely free from the usual stress, demands, and pressure of ministry life. A place where you're going to play, laugh, eat ice cream, and just be. Disneyland used to be this place for us. We could be out our front door and walking into Disneyland in less than two hours. Now that we live in Michigan, we haven't yet figured out what this "space" will be for us here, but we are excited to explore and find our new "Disneyland."

**6. Your spouse is not your mandatory ministry volunteer.** My husband loves youth ministry and teenagers, but he is not a mandatory volunteer, nor am I a two-for-one deal. I used to think the two-for-one deal worked in my favor. However, "Hire me because I come with a husband who will help lead the boys" is not an effective way to champion or lean confidently into your own calling as a woman in youth ministry. Yes, doing ministry together can be fun. But if a church is hiring you, they need to be hiring only you. This frees up your husband to serve and lead in the ministry areas where he is gifted and called to serve. Plus, what if your spouse isn't called to youth ministry? He might want to start up a men's basketball ministry and not be forced to be a middle school small group leader.

**7. Divide and conquer.** My husband and I don't have "assigned" gender roles in our family. We both do whatever needs to be done if we're able to do it. If he's home before me, he starts dinner. If he can stay home with a sick kid, he does. We tackle the demands of each day, week, and weekend together, contributing and pitching in however we can. If one

> Don't assume that because you thrive on middle school mayhem, your spouse does too. We are each made by God to do something for the kingdom, but we're not all made to do youth ministry. My husband mans the grill and takes out endless bags of trash like a champ when there are teenagers at our house. He gives teens rides to and from events, and he takes care of our own two children whenever I'm working on the weekends. But lead a small group of seventh grade boys in a six-week study of Philippians while simultaneously dodging Nerf darts? Not his thing. He loves people well and serves in his own ways. So I never assume he'll participate in a youth ministry event just because he's my husband. This allows him the freedom to serve in his own ways, and it also allows more peace and understanding in our relationship.
>
> —*Heather Henderson*

night the diapers, dishes, laundry, cooking, and baths need to be handled by my husband, he does it. Likewise, if I'm available to do those things, then I do them. We equally share in the responsibilities of the home. There are things he does better than I do and vice versa (like combing our daughters' hair after a bath). But whether or not it's done perfectly, it counts and it helps the family. Now, sometimes I'm better equipped to do certain things, like taking care of the baby's late-night feedings. (My husband wasn't designed to breast-feed a baby, and he's an incredibly heavy sleeper.) But then he'll pitch in by doing early morning diaper changes or holding the infant so I can take a shower in peace. We equally put in 100 percent.

**8. Tend to your own soul.** I am not the Holy Spirit to my husband, nor am I his personal trainer. We don't police each other's food intake ("Really, honey? Isn't that a bit large for a serving of ice cream?") And we don't police each other on the regularity of our own personal quiet times either. I do know that the whole Fruit of the Spirit thing is true. If I am walking closely with the Lord and spending time in prayer and Bible study, my Love, Joy, Peace, Patience, Kindness, Goodness, Faithfulness, and Self-Control quotient goes up exponentially.

Suddenly I am a better wife and a better mom. When I am tending to my own soul it's easy to notice. I am much more enjoyable to be around.

# QUESTIONS FOR REFLECTION

1. Where is your happy place "away from it all" to enjoy with your spouse or family?

2. Do you and your spouse margin in your day to refuel, relax, and connect so you are not run ragged by the weekend?

3. How are household chores and responsibilities divided in your family?

4. Does your husband volunteer in your youth ministry? Why or why not?

5. If so, what challenges do you face having your husband involved in the youth ministry with you?

6. Have you ever had to make a decision about whose job to pursue or had to move for the other one to get their "dream job?" Share your story.

7. What thoughts and experience do you have regarding couples who work or attend two different churches?

8. How are you going to be intentional this week to have downtime to relax with your spouse before the weekend?

9. If your theology of women in ministry leadership is complementarian or egalitarian, does that mean your marriage has to be too? Should it be? Why or why not?

# 13

# (YOUTH) MINISTRY NEEDS MOMS

Having babies when you're a female youth worker or ministry volunteer can be the best thing ever, and it can also seem like a lot to manage. Let's assume you are married and ready to have some kids. Can you be a great mommy and a great youth worker?

I want you to know that it can be done—and done really well. Our kids have only benefited from being a part of a youth group family. Jenna, my now nine-year-old, took her first steps in a church hallway while a teenager in my youth group held her hand. The teenagers and volunteer leaders have also benefited. They see a very incarnational example of what a Christian family looks like, and they get to do life with us. Real life with meltdowns, occasional grumpy days, and our kids playing the church drums when they know they aren't supposed to.

Staff and students eat at our dinner table, watch *America's Got Talent* with us (we even have our own buzzers), and observe us missing our little ones when we're away at camp. And our kids have a church family who cheers them on. With teenagers and volunteers loving on our children as we love on them, we all experience the most beautiful example of community I've ever seen. Having kids has only made me a better youth worker. I'm quite sure that being a youth worker has made me a more fun mom as well! Who else would bring a home a pile of foam finger rockets and goggles to try?

## ALL MOMS ARE WORKING MOMS
### BY APRIL DIAZ

I'm not going to lie. My kids are crawling all over me, asking for kisses, and demanding my full attention as I attempt to write this (after my deadline). This is real life for a momma in leadership.

For many years I didn't want to be a mom because I'd concluded that it was a game ender for me in ministry and leadership. Then, all I wanted was to be a mom (and figure out why we couldn't get pregnant even with the best medical help). Finally, we reclaimed our original dream of adoption, and seemingly overnight I became "Mom" to two toddlers from Ethiopia. Nine months later, I got pregnant. And by the time our youngest son arrived seven weeks premature, my husband and I had gone from zero to three kids in just 15 months.

In the meantime, my ministry position had moved into an executive leadership role, and my husband got laid off from his job. Oh, and we have no family living near us.

This opportunity to be a working mom in leadership has been one of the greatest challenges of my nearly two decades of ministry. Over the years God has graciously taught me a few things when it comes to being a working mom.

One of the first realizations was that we women can be our own worst enemies when it comes to our choices—and even theology—as working moms. *However, I am less than who God created me to be as a mom, wife, and woman in ministry when I believe the lie that I can do it all, all the time.* It's impossible for me to be an amazing wife, mother, friend, pastor, student, daughter, sister...*all day, every day.* The days when I place that expectation on myself are the days I feel the worst about myself. That's not the easy yoke Christ came to give me (Matthew 11).

Ultimately, I'm called to be a radical disciple of Jesus Christ! I've realized that I need to extend a LOT of grace to myself in this season of life with three young kids. And I'm pretty passionate about surrounding myself with people who will do the same for me. Parenting three little people is often exhausting even without the other responsibilities in my life. Thus, I've found that the people I'm drawn to the most are also those who are *foolishly graceful*. I want to be near these people because they will point me toward redemption and growth.

*I am also less than who God created me to be when I compare myself to other moms and their choices.* It's so easy to judge myself too harshly when I look at moms who stay at home and intentionally nurture their kids all day, every day. It's a lie when I believe those mommas' undivided attention is focused on their children's holistic development all day long. I know moms juggle a lot, regardless of their employment status. Making comparisons like this doesn't work, and it unfairly creates a villain and a hero out of those being compared.

Sadly enough, women can also be each other's worst enemies. I find that some women are brutally judgmental about the choices other women have made when it comes to raising children and working outside the home. We can be way too quick to judge another woman's circumstances:

- She is greedy (for prestige, money, appreciation...).

- She doesn't love her children as much as I love mine.

- She doesn't have much to offer outside the home.

- Her husband is controlling.

- Her husband is a pushover.

- She cares more about her career than her own children.

- She misinterprets Scripture and a woman's role in the family and church.

- She's only thinking about the short-term                                (or long-term) effects of her decision.

- She has to work because her husband doesn't make enough money.

Over the years I've discovered—usually the hard way—that it's far more mature and wise not to judge another mom's choices about work. More often than not, I don't know the whole story that's led to her decision. And for those times when I *do* judge and then learn the whole story afterward, repentance is in order.

I've learned that "to work or not to work" is a highly personal and emotional decision. The women I respect who also love Jesus passionately tend to make their decisions from a surrendered soul. They seek the voice of God for what their family needs.

My hope is that more women will pursue this all-too-important decision with the same prayerful and courageous spirit. I'm grateful for my dear friends who've gone before me in this endeavor. They've all chosen very different expressions of motherhood and work, but they've done so with thoughtfulness, prayer, and *ultimately* obedience to Jesus.

When you're a female (mom) youth worker standing at the front of a loud, fun, busy youth room filled with sugared-up, energetic teenagers, you get a lot of comments. I overhear words of encouragement or things like, "Wow! I could never do that!" from church friends as they pass by the youth room. But one reoccurring theme I've noticed over the years, in both large and small churches alike, is a familiar phrase spoken by young moms. I've heard it a lot. It goes something like this...

> *"Oh, wow! It's so great that you do youth ministry. I used to volunteer in youth ministry, back before kids. Maybe when my kids are in middle school, I'll help out in youth ministry again."*

I just smile and say, "We'd love to have you." But what I *really* want to share with these women, but never seem to have the time to do so during those quick moments, is...

"It's so worth it. I have a baby in the nursery right now, and doing youth ministry can totally work in a mom's schedule. Our teen girls would be so blessed to have moms like you serving on our volunteer team."

On my way to youth group this past Sunday, I walked by a couple of diaper bags and an infant car seat, and I just had to smile. Why? Because this adorable baby gear belongs to some of our youth group ministry volunteers. Women who had babies yet continue to serve in student ministry as small group leaders. Women who continue to love on teenage girls and, in turn, have a ton of teen girls (times 10) loving on their babies.

Babies sit on the floor at the back of the youth group room during our meetings. The teenagers beg to hold them and play peek-a-boo with them. These babies basically have their own fan club and cheering section. Sure it can be difficult at times, and occasionally it's even a bit distracting to have infants hanging out with teenagers during youth group programming. But isn't it a huge intergenerational win when teenagers, adults, and babies worship together?

When families continue ministering to teens even after babies come along, cool things happen. New moms and new dads who serve in youth ministry now take on a whole new level of "family ministry" opportunities.

We model with our lives and our time that teenagers matter to us, even when our stage of life changes after kids come along. And we allow teenagers to minister to us by loving our kids. Teens become big sisters and brothers to our own flesh and blood. They become an extra set of hands and an extra pair of eyes that look after our little ones who may be about to eat their fourth donut (because Mom isn't paying attention) or mess with those tempting knobs on the soundboard. There are teenagers who hold our kids when they cry or lift them high in the air to grab a balloon that got stuck on the youth room ceiling. They hold our little ones on their laps during a bonfire. Who is doing the real youth ministry here?

I realize some youth workers need to take a break and make self-care and family time a priority before stepping back into ministry. This is especially true if you work full time and need more time at home with your own kids. Yet, for those who continue on and don't take a break or stop serving once the baby arrives, the rewards are great. There are so many deep, rich, and full opportunities to care for teens as we step forward into all of life's changes (and baby blessings) with our students alongside us.

There are four thoughts I want you to consider before you pass up the chance to serve on a youth ministry team.

**1. Your kids will get their own cheering section.** The youth team, the teens in your church, and your super-stoked youth worker are all going to love you, and they're going to love on your kids even more. When my kids walk into the youth room, they're offered high-fives, hugs, cupcakes, and more love and community than they may have ever experienced otherwise. Volunteering in youth ministry shouldn't be done solely for the solicitation of a fan club for your kids. But inevitably, the more of your life that you share with the teens in your church, the more invested they will be in the life of your family. This can be a very good thing.

Recently, I pulled a diaper out of my baby's diaper bag, and guess what? There were little love notes written in Sharpie all over it. Yup, a sweet teenager who volunteers a lot in the church nursery had bestowed some "Sharpie love" all over a size 4 Pampers. I can't tell you how many teens from my various youth groups have taken the time to volunteer in my children's classes at church—and for the sole purpose of spending more time with my kids. My children have benefited so much. They have a church family and it rocks.

**2. Pay it forward.** Your kids will grow up and someday be in the youth ministry. Pour into the teens in your church right now and make a difference. Why wait to start or why stop volunteering just because you're having a baby? Be what you hope other adults will be for your own flesh and blood during their formative teenage years. Recent research from the Fuller Youth Institute confirms that for faith to last, adolescents need several adults in their church family to come alongside them and be a part of their lives in both little and big ways.[45]

This doesn't mean you trade raising your toddler for serving the teens in your church community, but maybe you can put in an hour or two each week to show teens they matter. Demonstrate a love for students and a love for Jesus through all of life's transitions and surprises. Providing consistent love, care, and investment into the teens in your church is a beautiful gift, and it can make a lasting impact in their lives.

**3. Moms are special.** Being a mom brings out a different kind of "mom love" for the teens in your church. As you begin to view students through the lens of motherhood, your ministry takes on an indescribable depth that might not have been there previously. Sure, I was a fantastic youth leader pre-kids, and no you don't have to be a parent to be an awesome youth worker. But I have a whole new and understandably different perspective now that I have kids of my own. It's one of those things you can't understand until you're on the flip side.

I do, however, have a lot less time. If I lacked any parental wisdom during my pre-kid youth ministry days, I made up for it by having loads more time for endless relational hours spent hanging out with teenagers. Youth ministry needs mom leaders because they have an optimism, patience, and nurturing way of doing ministry that your entire ministry will benefit from.

**4. You (probably) have the time.** You always have time for what's important to you. For instance, if yoga is important to you, you'll make time to do it. If you love youth ministry and are great with teenagers, then I hope you don't give it up just because your life got busier post-baby. Maybe you can't put in 40 hours a week or sign up to lead an epic three-day whitewater rafting trip this summer. But whether you've got 10 minutes or 10 hours a week to spare, I bet there are plenty of youth ministry opportunities available that will fit your schedule. Remember, a lot of youth ministry can be done alongside your family. So don't be afraid to invite teens into your everyday life experiences. Plus, it's always fun to hear teens oohing and aahing over your super cute baby.

When you're connected and invested in a faith community, you naturally want to serve in some capacity. Maybe it's in the children's ministry with your own kids, maybe it's in Awana or the women's ministry. But if youth ministry is your passion—your gift—then by all means keep at it! Using my gifts to serve the teens in our church has made me a better wife and a much more fun mom, and it's also strengthened my faith in a multitude of ways. If youth ministry is truly your calling, it's going to be something you'll want to keep doing through all of life's transitions.

So the next time you pass by the youth room and say, "I used to volunteer in youth ministry, back before kids," be warned: I might stop you in your tracks and hand you a volunteer application.

Whether you're a volunteer or paid youth pastor, you're going to need some time off from ministry after you have a baby. So how does that happen when you're leading a youth ministry? I've collected the following thoughts on the topic of maternity leave from two youth worker moms.

# MATERNITY LEAVE

Before I was a youth pastor, I was a public schoolteacher. And I think planning and taking a maternity leave, for any mom-to-be, is sort of like a teacher who creates lesson plans for a substitute so she can miss a few days of class. It's *so much work*, and it feels a little bit crazy!

The nuts and bolts of maternity leave will look different for everyone. My advice is, before you discover you're pregnant or adopting a child, find out if your church or organization has a maternity leave policy. They should, but they might not. (Mine didn't.) So you might have to work with your staff or team to figure it out. If you have the freedom, ask for some flexibility in the terms of your leave.

Know that there are things that won't get done while you're on leave. I'm an associate-level staff person, which means that when I went on maternity leave, there was still a full-time youth pastor working. Still, changes had to be made and some things went undone for a bit.

Prioritize and delegate. Be creative. It's tricky; but this is just a season, and it won't last forever. And when you return from leave, your work life will have to be adjusted. With a newborn at home, you may no longer be able to lead two midweek groups, plus teach or preach every Sunday. You probably shouldn't be doing all of that anyway. So delegate and empower others to lead as well. The ministry will be the better for it.

I had no clue how I was going to keep working 25 to 30 hours a week once my son was born. I have a preschooler, an infant, and a husband who is the CEO of an incredibly busy company. Plus, I'm supposed to do vocational youth ministry? Nevertheless, I believe God called me to youth ministry *and* to motherhood. So if this is God's plan for me, then I know he will help me navigate it. God is helping me, and he will help you too. Trust.

— *Heather Henderson*

Part of doing this well is accepting the fact that your male coworkers won't be able to fully understand what you're going through. Even if your home life goes against typical gender roles and your husband is primarily responsible for feeding the children, you're still the one going through pregnancy, labor and delivery, and recovery. Balancing parenthood—with new babies especially—and work will be a different experience for you than it is for your male coworkers.

However, your colleagues don't need to understand your experience in order to support you. Give them realistic expectations of what you can accomplish before, during, and after maternity leave. Work hard to enable your coworkers to do well both in your absence and after you return, but don't overcommit yourself. Knowing and creating your own limits will help your coworkers plan well, and it should also help limit their frustrations when you need to be with your family.

Remember, your unique experience of parenthood is one of your assets. Through the lens of a mom, you'll be able to understand, communicate with, and listen to your teenagers, their parents, and your ministry leadership better. Lean in to your experience as a mom. Don't forget that your perspective is needed and it's an asset to your team and your ministry.

— *Hannah Stevens*

I (Gina) have given birth to three kids and have gone through multiple miscarriages. Handling pregnancy, loss, maternity leave, and breast-feeding as a youth pastor has taught me a lot about myself and God's faithful provision. I've also learned about being more team-centered as I empower teenagers and adults to step into places of leadership and the roles I've had to give up in order to care for myself or an infant.

I've also experienced great love and support from the churches God has called me to. Every church has had a different (or nonexistent) maternity leave policy. So each time I had to meet with a supervisor or HR director to figure out a plan for the time I needed off. It wasn't easy, and it often presented financial challenges. But it always worked out in the end.

Going on maternity leave is a lot of work. Planning way ahead and handing off responsibilities to other staff or volunteers takes a lot of organization and brain space. The amount of work I did before maternity leave always seemed like twice as much work (because it is!) as it would have been if I'd just stayed and done it myself. Of course, once I was on my leave and enjoying time with a newborn, it was well worth it. All the crazy juggling, volunteer recruitment, and work I'd put into replacing myself during maternity leave proved worthwhile.

When you take time off after having a baby or recovering from a pregnancy loss, you will find that people from the wider church body are more than willing to step in and help. Some people who may not have volunteered otherwise will now offer to fill in. Youth group parents who don't normally participate will step up to help. And if you're lucky, they'll stick around even after you come back. As you learn to delegate and empower others for ministry, everyone wins.

Maternity leave forces you to learn more about recruiting, team building, and volunteer retention. It can be a wonderful learning experience that will only make you a better youth worker. You learn the beautiful lesson that youth ministry shouldn't be dependent on one person. It needs to be team driven.

Youth ministry needs to be embraced by the wider church community. As you release your ministry to others, you actually multiply the effectiveness of your own leadership. Maternity leave can be a wonderful part of your ministry experience and help you grow as a youth worker.

# QUESTIONS FOR REFLECTION

1. What challenges do you face (or worry about facing) as you seek to be a great mom and a great youth worker?

2. How do you know when it might be time to focus on your own family and make self-care a priority by stepping away from youth ministry for a while?

3. How can preparing for maternity leave increase your ministry recruiting skills?

4. How is being a mom an asset to your ministry and ministry staff?

5. What excites you the most about having a "youth group baby"?

6. How does the distraction of having a cute baby in the youth room trump a ministry without babies on board? Or does it?

7. Did anything in this chapter stand out to you or challenge your perceptions about being a mom in youth ministry?

# 14

# FIGURING OUT CHILDCARE AND FLEX TIME

As a woman working in full-time youth ministry for almost two decades, one question I'm often asked by both women in ministry and the caring pastors who employ them is, "How can a woman (in youth ministry) make the flexibility of youth ministry work for her when she has a child? What if she has no family in town to help?"

How do you handle childcare when you work full time? I've sat in Starbucks on many occasions with moms on maternity leave who are wrestling with this same question. Many panicked, wide-eyed, and stressed-out working moms feel a heavy tug from their work calendar and an even heavier tug toward staying home. So let me share a few ideas for creative childcare options, working from home, and last-minute sick days when you're a mom in youth ministry.

The best tip I learned after having my first baby is to take it one small chunk at a time. There is no way I can sit down and figure out a baby-sitting schedule for every single event. *Who will watch the kids during that mission trip two years from now?* If I tried to plan childcare for every youth event or trip on the horizon, steam would come out of my ears and I'd be driven insane with anxiety. Once I've found a baby-sitter, I can figure out day-to-day staff meetings and a generic weekly schedule fairly easily. But for the big trips and events, I've learned I have to just take it as it comes. One event and trip at a time. Somehow, it will work out!

So, do you need a baby-sitter? Is your maternity leave on the horizon and you're wondering what to do about childcare after the baby comes? What if you don't have extended family living nearby? I am 12 years into this full-time working mom thing, and I've had many creative childcare options come to fruition. Here are some solutions that might meet your childcare needs as well:

### 1. Trade Room and Board for a Live-in Nanny
This is what we did for child number one. We got wind of a girl who was living with a family in our church and helping them with childcare in exchange for room and board. Well, we had an extra bedroom. So when that family's needs changed, we offered her the same deal. She watched our baby Tuesday through Thursday. I worked from home one day a week and took my day off on Mondays. On youth group nights, we took the baby with us or put the baby in the church nursery. If that sort of arrangement doesn't work for you and you need to hire a paid nanny, take a look at *eNannySource.com*, *Care.com*, or ask around. There are many students at local Christian colleges who currently nanny or have friends who do.

### 2. Did You Say FREE?
Some women have a huge heart for youth ministry, love your church, love you, and want to help. They are typically people who love babies but don't want to volunteer in youth ministry with the *teenagers*. Over the years I've had many a trusted grandma or mom friend watch my baby for *free* while I ran a youth event or led a weekly staff meeting. (Usually they want to watch just one child, but they may be willing to watch two children, if you're lucky.)

Sometimes these women are youth group parents. So we'd basically trade children. I'd take her teen(s) with me to a youth event, and I'd leave my child at her house for free baby-sitting. This is an arrangement you can't expect or even ask for. You have to delicately and generically put it out there as a way that people could help the ministry. Or just wait until you get that "I'd love to watch your baby anytime" offer. Pray it up, put out some feelers, and of course be discerning. Not everyone is a good fit for watching your baby, so you need to be choosy. I'd like to take a moment right now to say thank you to Miss Karen, Miss Judy, Miss Sandi, Miss Maureen, Miss Paisley, Miss Julie, and all the other women who've invested in my family and ministry in this way.

### 3. Pay Teenagers
There were many years when I led both the junior high and senior high at a smaller church that didn't have a children's program or offer nursery care on the same night as youth group. That meant I couldn't just drop off my kids in another room at the church. And since my husband loves volunteering in youth ministry, he doesn't stay home to watch the kids unless he has to. At that time we lived super close to the church (i.e., in a parsonage on the same campus). So we decided to pay a senior high student to watch our kids during junior high youth group, and then we paid a trusted middle school student to watch our kids during senior high youth group. It's rare to find a really good sitter in middle school. So, again, be choosy! We were blessed to have a few "wiser than their years" students in our ministry who baby-sat our kids each week. (Yup, I'm talking about *you*, Katie and Emma!)

### 4. Craigslist
Did I really find reliable childcare on Craigslist? It seems awful to admit it, but I did! And it was a God thing. I found someone who seemed legit on Craigslist, but when I emailed her, I was surprised to discover that it was a woman from church whom I already knew and was friends with. I had replied to

my own friend's ad! Had we simply talked a little more at church, I would have found her that way. But it took God using Craigslist to make that connection happen. She watched my second baby from the time she was eight weeks old until she went to preschool. This should serve as a good reminder that God has your back.

### 5. Fish Around

My friend and I were on a walk one day, and she was talking about quitting her full-time job so she could stay home with her little one. She mentioned that she'd applied at Starbucks so she could make a little part-time money to supplement their family income. I was preggo with baby number three, and long story short: I supplement her income by paying her to watch my baby. She helps me out a ton with convenient and loving childcare, and she is one of my dearest friends! It is a win-win situation.

## IT DOES TAKE A VILLAGE

Parenting is hideously difficult yet exquisitely wonderful. And there is good news for all of us: We aren't meant to go this road alone! A passage of Scripture that gave me some freedom in this is found in Deuteronomy 6:4-9. It's often used to exhort parents to raise their children to follow God, which is great. But look at how that section of Scripture begins. It says, "Hear, O Israel," not "Hear, O parents." The whole clan is supposed to help bring up the little ones and raise them to love God. It's the work of a village!

— *Heather Henderson*

## THE INS AND OUTS OF MAKING A YOUTH MINISTRY SCHEDULE WORK

There are tons of options regarding working from home, taking your kids to the office, sick days, paid time off (PTO), having a flexible schedule, and so on. Every work and ministry environment has its own set of expectations and flexibility (or lack thereof). So make sure you and your employer are both clear about your needs and expectations regarding your work schedule, comp time, holiday pay, sick days, and office hours.

Also, I don't want to ignore the delicate subject of leaving the world of paid youth ministry to become a stay-at-home mom. That is an important decision to pray about and make when you aren't feeling irrational due to some raging postpartum hormones. Some women choose to step into a volunteer role so they can give as much as they want to ministry without the pressure of being on paid staff. When you aren't on the payroll, it's easier to say, "I can't be there tonight," or "I won't be able to attend summer camp this year."

I have friends who (temporarily) reduced their work hours so they could adjust to life with a newborn. However, I don't know if their ministry workload decreased that much (what with them being overachievers and all). Their guilty feelings

## THE BLESSINGS GO BOTH WAYS

I work at a smaller church, and we live far away from our families. It would be cost prohibitive to spend money on childcare just so my husband can serve as a volunteer in my youth ministry. Yet, God has provided for us in wonderful ways. I've been so blessed by the middle school girls who have served our family as mother's helpers. Many of the parents of our teenagers enjoy loving on our little ones and will baby-sit them during youth events. I also have a number of grandma types in the church who invest in the lives of our children. If someone you trust takes an interest in your kids, invite them to invest in your brood by baby-sitting and other ways. The sweet women who watch our kids so my husband and I can do youth ministry together have told us it's the highlight of their week—and it's the highlight of ours too!

— *Carmen Garrigan*

about working from home, coming into the office late, or going home early decreased a lot though. Reducing their hours helped them put less pressure on themselves to "do it all," and it also helped them ease back into full-time ministry at a comfortable pace.

I've spent more than a decade of my youth ministry career with what could be considered a flexible schedule. A *really* flexible schedule. I could work in the office for large chunks of time and bring a kid to work with me, I could work from home when needed, and I could also come in on Saturdays to make up any missed hours. I could also meet volunteers at a park or hang out with my students at the mall. Teen girls liked pushing the baby stroller through the mall, even when they got dirty looks from judgmental strangers. It was fun being able to invite teens and volunteers to dinner or bring my kids to events whenever I wanted to. Much of my youth ministry hours were spent outside of the office. And that's one of the things I love best about working or volunteering at smaller churches: It's much more natural and organic for ministry to overlap into many more opportunities for sharing life with teens, volunteers, and families.

What I discovered to be true is that this flexibility was often a trade-off or considered to be a sort of compensation. It was offered to me because the church wouldn't (or couldn't) pay me as much as I'd need to afford full-time childcare. They wanted what I had to offer professionally, and I wanted what they offered me personally (more time with my kids). The flexibility and untraditional schedule of a youth worker's life can work really well for youth worker mamas.

A flexible schedule for working moms is not a bad gig, especially for those eight years when I worked at a smaller church. I wouldn't trade those years for anything. A Working Mother 25th Anniversary Research report from IBM has this to say about flexibility on the job:

*There is a new recognition of the importance of viewing flexibility as a business tool versus individual accommodation...Leading companies realize that flexibility is not something just for women or working mothers, because men value flexibility too. Flex also increasingly has a role in attracting, retaining and motivating the multi-generational workforce—even occasional flex is highly valued by employees.*[46]

A flexible schedule is vital for working parents. Even if your schedule is only mildly flexible for days spent at home with sick kids or to chaperone an occasional school field trip, you will find that some wiggle room is necessary. Working in a large church setting with set office hours and less flexibility can work really well if it also provides more income and PTO (paid time off) than what smaller churches can offer. Competitive pay with benefits allows working mothers to handle the expense of full-time childcare. This kind of a ministry work environment with dedicated (non-kid) time and set office hours in which to focus professionally can help you be a better youth worker. It can help you be a much better parent too.

I've spent half of my youth ministry career working at a smaller church (under 200 members) and half of it at larger churches (over 3,000 members). Both worked well for me. Now that I'm working at a large church with a much less flexible schedule, I've discovered that when I'm working, I am "all in" when my kids aren't in the office with me. I also tend to be "all in" when I'm at home without work hanging over my head. Occasionally, when my husband is working late, I may need to pick up the older kids from school and stick them somewhere in the student room for an hour. But that's not the norm. For the most part, I work kid-free all week long, and it helps me keep my work and home lives more separate.

Large churches aren't necessarily anti-kid environments, but working there isn't like my days spent in small-church world where I could let my baby nap in the church nursery or let my daughter watch *Yo Gabba Gabba!* on repeat in my office while I worked. Once when my (then) two-year-old threw up all over my office, the senior pastor cleaned up my daughter's vomit so I could take her home more quickly. Now *that* is true servant leadership right there. That doesn't usually happen at megachurches.

Now that I've been working full time with regular office hours for more than five years, I love having my big kids in elementary school all day and my toddler in full-time daycare. Where I work now, the church office is closed to all on Fridays. This schedule helps me stay in the zone when I'm in ministry mode, and dialed in to my family at all other times. Everyone on staff works hard (and longer days) Monday through Thursday in order to have Fridays and Saturdays off. Of course, there are times when things come up, such as funerals or crisis counseling. And camps and retreats can suck up a weekend. But overall, my schedule is predictable and set. I don't drag myself into the office to finish undone tasks on a Saturday (nor does anyone else).

If your senior pastor and ministry colleagues rarely take their day off, come in every Saturday, and have terrible boundaries with their time, watch out. It's going to be difficult for you to have a healthy work schedule with set times for ministry and protected time for yourself, your marriage, and your family. Pay attention. If your colleagues are terrible workaholics, it will be tough for you to maintain good boundaries on your own time.

If you're interviewing for a youth ministry position somewhere, pay careful attention to how those on staff spend their time, their evenings, and their Saturdays. Ask your potential employer and others on staff what a typical week is like and get a sense for how they prioritize family over ministry in that work environment. Ask if they have vacation days and if they use them. If your kids end up hating church and walking away from Jesus, or if your spouse resents your job, then your ministry is not worth the cost.

Ministry is ministry, and of course there will be beautiful times when family and ministry collide in the shared space of our home, when I'm hanging out with volunteers or students at a park with my kids, or when my family comes along on a ministry trip (if it makes sense to bring them). This kind of overlap should be allowed to happen because teenagers and ministry staff need to see how families who follow Jesus interact, include, invite, and love on others.

# QUESTIONS FOR REFLECTION

1. Do you prefer a work environment where you can work from home, bring your baby to work, and "flex" your time? Or do you like a more traditional schedule? Why?

2. When is it helpful and beneficial to your ministry to have your kids and family around? When is it not?

3. What is your priority for family and days off in your current context? Does your supervisor model healthy time management? Does she or he take a day off?

4. Do you take a day off? Is that hard for you to do or have you managed your schedule to accommodate it?

5. If you have kids, how have you managed sick days and childcare so far? What makes your schedule work? What challenges have you faced?

6. How do you feel about using full-time daycare so you can work full time in youth ministry? Is this an option you would love or love to hate?

7. How might volunteering in youth ministry be a great option for moms who want to stay in youth ministry after having kids?

# 15

# BANANAS, BARF, AND BOOGERS IN YOUR HAIR (NO SICK DAYS FOR MOMS)

There are sick days (theirs), and then there are sick days (yours) when you're so sick that you wonder what you should do with your kids. Sometimes your only resort is to turn on the Disney Channel, put a box of Cheerios and a stack of juice boxes in the middle of the living room floor, and then collapse pitifully onto the sofa. Days with sick little ones aren't easy for anyone. Who can you call to come take care of your kids when you're barely alive? Do you ever wish moms could take a sick day from their mommy responsibilities? No one wants you around the office if you're sick and germ infested, but life at home doesn't stop just because you don't feel well. Thankfully, I don't get sick as often as my kids do.

I was vomited on twice and peed on once this very morning. Yes, I am home with a sick toddler as I write this. Mondays are my meeting days, so of course my daughter wakes up ill on a Monday. I called my boss. His gracious response: "Take care of your daughter. If you can work while you're at home, great. But do whatever you need to do to care for your daughter and take care of yourself so you don't get sick. We can figure out the hours later." I thank God for a boss who has kids and for PTO (paid time off).

I am part of a team, and when someone is out for a day or a few days, we are there to support and assist each other. Maybe you have a flexible schedule, an understanding supervisor, and PTO. Or maybe you don't. *How do you manage things when all hell breaks loose and you find yourself covered in barf?*

As a mom of three, I've spent a lot of time thinking about how to juggle motherhood and ministry. Having a child gives a working mom a lot to navigate and figure out. Sick days, even more so. After all, your baby never seems to spike an out-of-the-blue fever on your day off. The stress of balancing it all can drive you to want to quit your job and be a stay-at-home mom.

I vividly remember about a year and a half ago, Julia, my bouncing, wide-eyed, and ready-to-be-up-for-the-day baby, woke me up at 3 a.m., right in the middle of a dream about work. She was calling to me through the baby monitor. So I shuffled toward the girls' room. Julia shares a room with her big sister Jenna. So when baby comes calling through the airwaves, I am quick to jump out of bed before she wakes her sister. Feeling groggy and with my hair a mess, I picked up the baby and we headed back to my room. I attempted to nurse/snuggle/nurse her, hoping she'd fall back asleep. It worked for a bit until my now-mobile 20-pound baby attempted to stand up and bounce on the mattress.

With a loud, awake, and very wiggly baby, I headed downstairs and tried to get her to sleep in her Pack 'n Play, while I drug a pillow and blanket to the sofa so I could hopefully sleep nearby. Nope. She shrieked every time I set her down. So I picked up the shrieking baby and retried my nurse/snuggle/nurse routine on our sofa. We both fell asleep for about a half hour until she started playing with my...well, let's just say "milk dispenser"...while standing on the sofa. To make a long story short...it was a very long night!

Eventually, both mama and baby fell asleep. I think a six-ounce bottle of milk from the fridge was involved. I was desperate and did the no-no of sticking her back in the Pack 'n Play with a bottle of milk in her mouth. My pediatrician has scary pictures of babies with tooth decay caused by going to bed with a bottle. For a moment, I imagined Julia with metal caps on her teeth when she's three, and then I shrugged my shoulders.

After a long night with a too-awake baby, I wake up to hear my other blond-haired, blue-eyed beauty begging me to let her stay home from school today. "I feel like I am going to throw up."

I reply, "You're just tired. Please try to go to school." I remind her it's picture day and her hair is looking good. I begin to secretly panic as I think about *my* day. Yes, it's Wednesday— youth group day! It's also staff meeting day, and there's a big fall outreach event tonight. It's a big fat busy day. "Please, please, try to go to school; and if you are really sick, I can pick you up." Nope. That didn't work. Tears started flowing down her sweet face, so I grabbed the thermometer to see how sick she really was.

Dang. A fever. She really was sick. Oh, what is a working mama to do? I turned to my husband who was eating a bowl of cereal before he had to head for work. "What is the earliest you can be home?" He is a teacher, and sometimes in a pinch he can get out early if he doesn't have an afternoon class. He reminded me that he had flag football that day (he was the coach), and their first game was after school.

"Six o'clock," he replied. Oh. Great. That sucks. The busiest day ever with one sick seven-year-old, a tired baby who needed to go to the sitter, and a 10-year-old boy who had to be picked up from school at the exact same time as my staff meeting. And I had no help. Not yet anyway. Can you feel the stress level rise?

I dialed my usual backups—my mom and my grandma. My grandma was nowhere to be found. Eventually she called me back from the DMV. She'd been there all morning and couldn't leave yet. I hung up the phone and started to feel more overwhelmed. I was seriously questioning this whole working full time thing. My mom was at work and couldn't get to my house until 5 p.m. So I decided to work from home for as long as I could, take the baby to the sitter's house, and then drag my poor feverish girl to my office and let her sleep on my sofa.

Once I arrived at the sitter's house with baby Julia in tow, she and I started chatting about her mother-in-law who'd had a fever for several days. I told her Jenna also had a fever and was staying home from school with me. I admit I got a little teary-eyed with the stress of everything weighing heavily on my shoulders. I felt guilty for not being able to stay home.

Well, being the awesome neighbor friend that she is, she offered to keep Jenna for me too. Then my mom came over after work and watched the kids until my husband got home. Crisis averted and all was well in the world

Youth group happened and we had a fantastic outreach event! A few unchurched boys from my campus club attended. They ran up to me and said, "Hi, Miss Gina, we came!" And there was a good response to the gospel message of hope that was shared. Being a mom in full-time youth ministry definitely has its tough days, but somehow it all works out. It just does.

Walking into work this past Tuesday, I overheard one of our executive pastors talking about how he'd stayed home on Monday with his little boy who was ill. I'd also stayed home on Monday with a vomiting two-year-old. As he took a sip of his coffee, he shared, "When a kid gets sick, you have about a 10-minute window to talk about who has the busier day and decide which parent is going to stay home." I took comfort in his words because his reality was also my reality. We live parallel lives. We both work on pastoral staff, we're married to teachers, and we're raising school-age kids. He added, "It's so much work for a teacher to put together plans for a sub. So if I can clear my schedule and work from home, I do. If I can't, she does."

I've seen how an egalitarian hermeneutic for marriage and ministry directly impacts the work atmosphere and positively impacts home life for all. The men who serve as executive pastors at my church are okay with staying home with their sick kids. That's why I work here. That's the kind of church I want to raise my kids in.

I remember a wise and witty lady named Monica who worked on a Christian education committee with me during my Presby days. As she was heading out the door one day to get back to her family, she said: "When the kids are sick and life has to stop, I take it as God's way of telling me to slow down." I've never forgotten those words. It's time to pause the committees, the volunteering, the workload, and the crazy pace of life and just slow down for a bit. You have to make youth ministry work with your life—not let it run your life.

# QUESTIONS FOR REFLECTION

1. How might working for a ministry supervisor who has kids be helpful?

2. How do you handle sick days? Do you have PTO? A flexible schedule?

3. What does team ministry have to do with sick days? Why is it essential to empower and equip others to lead your ministry?

4. How do your ministry supervisors react to sick days (yours and theirs)?

5. Has there been a time when you had to scramble to pull off a youth event and manage an illness (your own or your child's)? What happened?

6. What tips do you have for keeping yourself and your family (if you have one) healthy?

7. When do you know your crazy pace of life requires time for a "sick day" or a PTO "mental health" day?

8. When you were a kid, how did your parents handle sick days? Did Mom or Dad stay home with you or call Grandma?

9. What challenged you in this chapter? What ideas or encouragement did you glean?

# 16

# MISSION TO MARS (FAILURE AND THE JOB OF YOUR DREAMS)

It was a regular Tuesday morning in the church office. It was a cooler than usual Southern California day, so as I gathered my wallet, I put on one of my many youth ministry sweatshirts. I paused my Spotify mix, shut my office door, and left the student ministry offices as I headed across the street to the main church campus. A nice well-worn path exists between my office and the church coffee bar. Only one crosswalk, two sets of stairs, and a busy parking lot separate this girl from her nonfat double latte with extra foam.

The street was unusually empty for this time of day, except for a middle-aged woman driving an SUV. She was speeding down the road and headed in my direction. I hit the crosswalk button on the stoplight. As the car continued to speed quickly toward the intersection, she noticed that her light had turned yellow and then red. She gave me the evil eye, put the pedal to the metal, and flipped me off as she ran the red light. Slowing down to let me cross the street was by no means an option in her mind. She wanted to speed through the light and was furious that I'd hit the crosswalk button and changed her light to red. Slowing down was the last thing she wanted to do, so she didn't.

When a light you expected to stay green suddenly turns red, do you react in angst or do you take it as a sign that you need to sit still a moment and slow things down? Is it the time to get impatient and upset, or a time to reevaluate and reflect? Do you get mad, or do you sit back and patiently wait for the green light? This woman who'd flipped me off in a church crosswalk gave me a lot to ponder. No one likes to slow down, but sometimes we don't have a choice. And sometimes it's an unexpected gift.

I'd been reflecting on the way I experienced ministry back when I worked at a Presbyterian church. I missed working at a place where I could have a professional lunch with a male coworker, drink wine with dinner, and preach a sermon on Sunday morning. I was growing more and more unsettled with the theology of my present context and the limitations it placed on me. It was time to slow down and seek God's next steps for me. Red lights were everywhere, warning me that it was time to stop and figure out an alternate route.

I remember sitting in a planning meeting for a well-known middle school conference with a bunch of other middle school pastors. We were all interested in bringing this conference to our area. During the meeting one of my (male) supervisors mentioned that our church couldn't host the conference if a female was the speaker. Wow...a talented, well-known female middle school pastor from Minnesota was part of the lineup for this particular conference. So now we couldn't host the conference if she was chosen to speak in our city? Many of the other youth workers thought that was dumb and voiced their opinions. I thought it was stupid too, but I didn't say anything because my bosses were hosting this meeting at my church. Their theology informed my paycheck and speaker choices.

I was really sick of the gender thing, and I could tell it wasn't going to go away. When a female was booked to be the speaker during the weekend winter camp that our high schoolers were scheduled to attend, the high school youth pastor had to call the camp and ask them to either change our camp dates or book a male speaker instead. How dumb. Especially when more than half (80 percent, actually) of those going to winter camp were female students. The gender bias was obvious to me, and I wasn't okay with it anymore. Their theology informed my speaker selection.

Our senior pastor used the pulpit to let us all know how important it was to vote our values. I thought of my high school friend Lissa. You remember Lissa. She's the one who introduced me to Barbara, the first female youth worker I'd ever met. Well, my sweet friend Lissa had bravely told me that she's a lesbian. "I'll understand if you don't want to be friends anymore," she'd said, as we sat on a bench overlooking the Pacific Ocean. I sure didn't want my church's political zeal to be a stumbling block to her faith or get in the way of her experiencing the unconditional love of God. Yes, vote your values, but don't use the pulpit to promote politics that may alienate the very people you're trying to reach. "Of course I still want to be your friend," I said. Their theology informed the way I invited (or didn't invite) my friends to church.

I no longer wanted to enforce the dress code and excessive modesty rules as part of my youth ministry job. Dress-coding always came at the expense of shaming and damaging the female teens I was called to love and serve. I was no longer willing to share with a student how much "God loves you" and then dress-code her for exposed bra straps or wearing a two-piece bathing suit. Especially not when we allowed our good-looking muscular male youth staff to parade around without their shirts on during summer swim parties. The real message we were sending was "God loves you...so long as your shorts are not too short, and you don't talk to our incredibly attractive (and shirtless) male volunteers for extended lengths of time." Theology informed my job description with damaging dress-code rules I had to enforce.

## AND THEN I FAILED...

As I continued to question my theology, my call, and my longevity in "Left Behind" world, I started to keep my eyes open for something better. I applied for my dream middle school pastor job at a church where I really wanted to work. Like, run to my computer, call my BFF, and jump up and down with glee because this particular church was hiring a middle school pastor. And this church was okay with hiring female pastors. I made sure to get my résumé to them ASAP.

I didn't get the job. I came close. Really close. But I didn't make the final cut, and it sucked. They never did fill the position due to a hiring freeze...but if they had, it wasn't going to be me. I was bummed. It felt awful to be so close to getting the one job I really wanted. So I stayed a little longer where I was. However, not getting that job made me work harder to become a sought-after, high-capacity job candidate for when the next opportunity rolled around.

## AND THEN I QUIT...

I eventually quit my big church youth ministry job without having another job lined up. I could have stayed in megachurch world...the people pleaser in me was willing to keep the people happy. I could toe the company line, be okay with not being the pastor in charge of the ministry, hide my real thoughts, and so on. But it wasn't healthy for me to be what I wasn't.

I needed the paycheck and health benefits, which made it tougher for me to leave even though I knew it was for the best. But I decided (in faith) to leave because it was clear I wasn't a good fit there. My theology wasn't what it used to be when I was an 18-year-old intern and just beginning my ministry at the very church I was now leaving almost 20 years later.

# NOT GETTING THE JOB YOU WANT

After my freshman year of college, I knew I wanted to intern at my church. I hadn't been asked to do it; I just knew that's what I wanted to do. So I went to the church leadership over my spring break and asked for a job. I was told no. It hurt. No one likes rejection—not even when they understand why they're being rejected. I wish I could say I joyfully understood and went home praising Jesus with Hillsong blaring through my open car windows. But instead, I left there feeling confused as to why God had put this desire on my heart just so I could step out in faith and feel embarrassed and insecure about being told no.

But then I was offered a job at one of the community campuses of my church, a smaller campus with 60 students or so—completely different than the megachurch I was used to. They told me about the size of the youth group, that the church met in a high school, and that I'd have a pretty small budget. Terrified of the unknown, I said I'd "pray on it." After all, I was also considering another option to help at a Christian camp that summer.

Well, God being God, he changed my heart. I took the job and fell in love. I fell more in love with ministry, I fell in love with the community, and I was thrilled to have a job where I get to grow exponentially as a girls minister. It wasn't what I'd planned to do, and it was terrifying. Goodness knows I still have no idea what I'm doing half the time! But it's my home, it's my church, and they're my students.

Being rejected hurts, and we always hear clichés about God's plan whenever it happens to us. But what if instead of sulking after a rejection, we found a way to rejoice in the hope we have and pray for the patience we need?

— *Chelsea Peddecord*

# THEN CAME NOW

Failure is not final. After I didn't get that dream job I really wanted, I spent those 18 months developing myself. Instead of thinking, *Oh, poor me*, I used that "no" to grow and become the best I could be in my field. I grew professionally—I read a lot, wrote, and thought through my theology. I read *The Blue Parakeet* by Scot McKnight and outgrew my "ministry associate" title. I was ready to be a ministry pastor. To live into the reality of all God had made me and called me to be. I didn't want my gender to hold me back when I could lead, speak, and preach just as well as "the boys." I failed forward. Failure made me better. I wanted to work at a place where my theology informed my paycheck, speaking selection, book selection, and dress code in a healthier way.

In the summer of 2013, my dream church was (again) hiring a middle school pastor. The job was reposted on their website, which I'd been stalking quite often. They remembered me from the last time I'd applied, and they fast-tracked my résumé to the top of the pile. After a whirlwind of Skype interviews and email exchanges, I was in Grand Rapids with my husband for an on-site interview weekend. The previous weekend I'd been in Atlanta interviewing at a Presbyterian megachurch for a job pastoring young families. Two big job possibilities were before me. My husband and I had a lot to consider and pray about.

Thankfully, that weekend we spent in Atlanta had made three things clear:

1. I don't care for the humidity in the South or being called "ma'am." (Sorry, Southerners!) But I do love the Waffle House.
2. I wasn't ready to give up doing youth ministry just so I could get paid a nice income and hang out with young moms and babies.
3. I still love Presbyterians, but I am definitely not one.

I *love* youth ministry, which I think became unmistakably obvious to the executive pastor in Atlanta who was interviewing me. I was much more comfortable chatting up her teenagers (who are in high school) than I was talking with the young couples I was supposed to be wowing with my conversational skills.

After an interview dinner at her home, my husband and I looked at each other. We were like, *Crap, what are we doing here?* When you're called to youth ministry, it's a lifelong calling. A calling that supersedes your age, your pay, your stage of life, or your marital status. It's a calling you don't want to leave. My husband and I wanted to be like Bart and Connie. We wanted to someday be grandparents who volunteer and lead a high school small group in our living room. You're never too old to do youth ministry.

The possibility of working on staff at the largest Presbyterian church in the country (with a really nice paycheck) was appealing. *Really* appealing. Yet, I couldn't shake the fact that it was a young family ministry pastor position. It wasn't youth ministry. It wasn't my life's calling. And it wasn't for me.

So there we were at the church in Michigan. The same place that had originally turned me down for the middle school ministry pastor job. It had been less than five days since our interview weekend in Atlanta. And the contrast between the two churches made it abundantly clear that we'd found our people. Our tribe. I was smitten with Michigan, the church, and the Great North.

Toward the end of the interview weekend, one of the executive pastors looked at me and said, "Gina, I've noticed you use the job title 'youth worker' a lot. I'd like you to stop saying 'youth worker' and start using the word 'pastor.' You are a *pastor*, and you need to get comfortable calling yourself a pastor." I used to think titles didn't matter much...I'm not so sure about that anymore! I've discovered that when a church is willing to call you what you are—a *pastor* to students—you get your voice back.

Then came the moment I could have only hoped for, and it was just a few hours before our flight back to San Diego. I was offered the job. An envelope with a job offer was presented to me and placed in my hands. I was floored. My dreams were coming true. I had found my church home. And then I did cry.

*It's funny how some distance makes everything seem small*
*And the fears that once controlled me can't get to me at all*
*Up here in the cold thin air, I finally can breathe*
*I know I left a life behind, but I'm too relieved to grieve.*[47]

Now it's 2014 and here we are in Michigan. I'm living my dream as a full-time middle school ministry pastor. Every once in a while, I walk down the hallway in what is now my church home, and I say to myself, *I am here!* And I thank God for choosing me to be here and work as a woman in youth ministry. When you lean in to your calling and live your life with all of its disappointments, failure, and fallout, you must continue on. It might just be the beginning of a better story.

*And the cold never bothered me anyway.*

# QUESTIONS FOR REFLECTION

1. How do you know when it's time to stay or leave a ministry position?

2. What is your "dream" youth ministry job (paid or volunteer)?

3. Have you ever wanted a job so bad and gotten close only to receive the "thanks, but no thanks" phone call or email? How did that feel?

4. How do you handle no?

5. How does failure make you better?

6. Have you ever been forced to slow down or rethink your calling when you didn't want to?

7. Does a call to youth ministry ever go away?

8. When is youth ministry a lifelong calling and when is it a "just for right now" opportunity?

9. What's your ministry story? How did you get where you are right now?

# 17

## GETTING CHICKED

It was one of those dumb things you do after eating too many Christmas cookies and gaining winter weight: I decided to start running. I'd made a New Year's resolution to show up early on Saturday mornings and run with a "mentor" who would coach me all the way to a 25K…one step at a time. I spent a few hundred dollars on winter running gear. I bought the waterproof running shoes. I bought the thermal running pants, neck gaiter, and reflective jacket. And then I ran for the first time since…? Probably high school gym class.

There I was in a downtown park on an early Saturday morning. Dave, an old man recovering from knee surgery, ran with me. He talked to me about form and encouraged me to keep running. He'd run marathons. I'd run the four blocks to Starbucks. That January morning we did three miles. In the snow. He didn't mind how slow I was because did I mention he was recovering from knee surgery? Slow was his new normal.

As Dave and I ran, he looked over at me and said, "You know, women used to not be allowed in this sport. Back when I started, women weren't allowed to run. Things have really changed. There are a lot of women running these days." He continued to run next to me for a bit, and then he said, "What you'll find here is a community of runners, male and female, who really support each other. Some people are not into the camaraderie; but if you want it, it's here." It was true. Everyone clapped and cheered for us as they ran by. Gracious and experienced runners lapped me twice. It totally felt like high school, where I was always the last runner in. But with nicer people. And they all knew Dave.

What Dave said about women in the sport of running stuck with me. I'd never really thought about running as a man's sport. I had no idea it used to be that way. Then I thought back to the early days of the Olympic games when women weren't allowed to participate. In ancient Greece, married women couldn't even watch the games. If they did, the penalty was death. As I looked into the history of women runners, I learned that in 1967, Katherine Switzer registered for the Boston Marathon as K. Switzer in order to get a number. She hid her feminine features by putting her hair up in a hat and wearing a giant sweatshirt. After the gun went off, she took off the sweatshirt and hat and began running the race. A Boston Marathon official, a man named Jock Semple, yelled at her to stop and attempted to rip off her number. Later in life he reversed his position and became one of the strongest supporters of women in the sport.[48]

I couldn't stop thinking about one story I read in an article called "Getting 'Chicked'–A History of Women's Running":

*Even through the 1960s and into the '70s, American women were taught that running was a man's sport. One friend I've made as a professional runner is a woman who was one of America's finest pioneers of the sport and the first American woman to break 4:40 in the mile.*

*One night before a race, I stayed the night at her house and listened to her stories of running in Seattle in the*

*'60s when both men and women would throw things at her as she was running and even physically push her off of trails. This was a very tough time for women in the sport, but then the '80s happened.*[49]

I was out there in the snow after making an overly ambitious New Year's resolution. I found myself, a woman, running with older runners, younger runners, experienced ones, novice ones. Male runners. Female runners. I didn't know it wasn't always this way… that inclusion was the new norm. Running is now a common experience filled with camaraderie, support, cheering, and mentors looking out for the slower ones. Their motto is "no runner left behind."

What I didn't realize at first is that not everyone was training for a 25K. Some were training for a 10K. Some for a 5K. Everyone was self-aware enough of their own athletic abilities and ambitions to pick the race that was the best fit for them. A recipe for success, not frustration.

My challenge for women in youth ministry is to run *your* race, not someone else's. As you discover your own leadership and ministry gifts, run your race. Find places to serve and volunteer that fit your theology and don't hinder the path God has for you. I am not Dave. I am not a marathon runner. I am a five-foot-short, mildly out-of-shape woman who's more fit for a 5K than a 25K. I know my gifts, weaknesses, and what kind of "running" lifestyle fits into my current family context. Early morning long runs on Saturdays are not for me. I'd rather hang out with my kids in their PJs and drink coffee all morning. However, after-work long walks with my husband totally fit. We leash up the dog, put the two-year-old in the stroller, and walk. This fits my life, my rhythm, and my lifestyle. It's me being *me* instead of purchasing hundreds of dollars worth of running gear to be someone I am not.

Ministry is like this. I think of Brittany who leans in to her leadership with a much more hierarchical-complementarian church and navigates it so well. Nothing is holding her back, and she confidently lives her life leading, loving, and volunteering in a context that fits who she is. I think of Carmen, my Presbyterian BFF who has never known anything different than a ministry lifestyle with an abundance of female pastors and female head of staff to work with and work for. I think of Mariah who is in her early 20s and leading an entire youth ministry. I think of myself who started out in a really conservative ministry environment and needed to evolve and change ministry contexts to match my expanding view of women in youth ministry. I think of Sonia, Connie, and Barbara, who all have "real jobs" and do this youth ministry thing on the weekends and on Wednesday nights.

One day I invited Sami (not her real name), a 20-year-old volunteer, over for lunch. We sat at my dinner table and talked about youth ministry. She wasn't sure if she should continue volunteering as a small group leader in our youth group. She was being pressured by an on-campus parachurch ministry to step it up and invest more of her time in a leadership role there. It was a college ministry in which Sami didn't think she could completely be herself or ask honest questions without them questioning her theology or her understanding of the gospel. They also didn't think serving as a girls' small group leader in the local church was where she should be spending her time, when serving her college community was (in their opinion) a better option. After all I've learned in my 15+ years of ministry, I gave her this advice:

> *Sami, lead where you can use all of your gifts for ministry to the fullest extent. Minister in the place that fits your theology, your college life, and your schedule in the best way possible. When it's a burden, when it's not fun, and when you can't use your gifts or be yourself, then maybe it isn't a good fit. I support you, and I want you to serve in the place that fits your life*

*the best right now. Maybe it's campus ministry, maybe it's not. But serve where you can lead, grow in your faith, and be* you.

My challenge to Sami is my challenge to all of us: Figure out your theology, your gifts, and what fits into the rhythm of your life right now. Serve in the places and with the people who allow you to step fully into your calling and be yourself.

Be the woman God created you to be and remain faithful to the theological limitations or freedoms you hold based on your own hermeneutic of women in leadership. Do what fits your schedule and your family. Run your race and follow your calling, not someone else's. Be an encourager of those out on the ministry trail who may be doing things differently than you.

I don't know if Dave was happy "back in the day" about women participating in his sport (although, I'm pretty sure he is a fan of inclusion). But regardless, on that cold January day, he supported and encouraged this wannabe chick runner, and together we ran three miles. That's something I haven't done since I was in PE class with Lissa back in 1995.

So lead. Love your calling. Live *your* life—not someone else's—and remember we are women and men who may be running different races, but we must never forget that we're all on the same team.

# QUESTIONS FOR REFLECTION

1. Have you ever signed up for something or declared a New Year's resolution and later wondered what the heck you'd gotten yourself into? What happened?

2. How can trying to be something you're not hinder you from leaning in to your calling and living the life you're called to lead?

3. How is ministry like my 25K race story? Does youth ministry have to be all or nothing?

4. How can you encourage others in youth ministry who come from a different theological framework or denominational background than you?

5. Are you more like a Brittany, a Mariah, a Carmen, or a Gina?

6. As you think about running, look at 1 Corinthians 9:24-27 and examine your own race (not someone else's). How's it going?

# ENDNOTES

[1] Ruth Moon, "Christian College Solidifies Complementarian Stance," Gleanings: Theology, *Christianity Today*, posted March 21, 2014, http://www.christianitytoday.com/gleanings/2014/march/christian-college-solidifies-complementarian-cedarville.html.

[2] Veronica Roth and Emma Galvin, *Divergent* (Unabridged. ed.) (New York: Harper Audio, 2011).

[3] NPR, "'Lean In': Facebook's Sheryl Sandberg Explains What's Holding Women Back," posted March 11, 2013, www.npr.org/2013/03/11/173740524/lean-in-facebooks-sheryl-sandberg-explains-whats-holding-women-back.

[4] Pantene Philippines, "Labels Against Women," November 9, 2013, www.youtube.com/watch?v=kOjNcZvwjxI.

[5] John Trent and Gary Smalley, *The Treasure Tree* (Dallas: Word Publishing, 1992).

[6] The Enneagram Institute, "8 The Challenger: Enneagram Type Eight," www.enneagraminstitute.com/TypeEight.asp.

[7] The Myers & Briggs Foundation, "More About Personality Type," www.myersbriggs.org/more-about-personality-type/.

[8] Ezra Klein, "Competent Women Are Getting Bypassed by Overconfident Men," Vox, posted May 5, 2014, www.vox.com/2014/5/5/5683196/competent-women-bypassed-by-overconfident-men.

[9] Ibid.

[10] Sheryl Sandberg, *Lean In*, 25.

[11] Mark DeVries, "The End of Paid Youth Ministry?" *Group Magazine* (May/June 2014).

[12] http://www.youtube.com/watch?v=KmmGClZb8Mg

[13] Veronica Roth, *Divergent* (New York: HarperCollins, 2011), 223.

[14] National Network of Youth Ministries, www.nnym.com/index.cfm/fuseaction/home.myhome.

[15] Tweeted by Matt Laidlaw on 11.15.2013.

[16] Bold Boundaries: Expanding Friendship Between Men and Women Conference, A Sacred Friendship Gathering, "Bold Boundaries" webpage, http://sacredfriendshipgathering.com/.

[17] Sheryl Sandberg, *Lean In*, 77.

[18] Emily Maynard, "Modesty: Asking Not Telling," *Emily Is Speaking Up* blog, posted July 8, 2013, www.emilyisspeakingup.com/blog/2013/7/8/modesty-asking-not-telling.

[19] Sheryl Sandberg, *Lean In*, 72.

[20] David Hayward, "Silence as Key to Pastor Dad Mark Driscoll's Ministry," *NakedPastor* blog, posted September 10, 2013, www.patheos.com/blogs/nakedpastor/2013/09/silence-as-key-to-pastor-dad-mark-driscolls-ministry/.

[21] Brené Brown, *Men, Women, and Worthiness: The Experience of Shame and the Power of Being Enough, Audio Book* (Sounds True, November 15, 2012), www.brenebrown.com.

[22] Bold Boundaries: Expanding Friendship Between Men and Women Conference, A Sacred Friendship Gathering, "Bold Boundaries" webpage, http://sacredfriendshipgathering.com/.

[23] Rachel Blom, "Life as a Youth Worker: An Interview with Dan Crouch," Churchleaders.com, www.churchleaders.com/youth/youth-leaders-blogs/159280-rachel_blom_life_as_a_youth_worker_an_interview_with_dan_crouch.html.

[24] http://cashboardapp.com/

[25] www.myersbriggs.org/my-mbti-personality-type/mbti-basics/

[26] www.enneagraminstitute.com/

[27] This refers to a movement developed and championed by the Fuller Youth Institute. For more information, check out http://stickyfaith.org/.

[28] WSJ Digital Network, "Inside Look at Google's New York Offices," posted February 28, 2012, http://www.youtube.com/watch?v=bpm_LIyMtMY.

[29] Mars Hill Bible Church Mission Statement

30 The CWA was founded as Beverly LaHaye's response to the feminist movement in America during the late 1970s. www.cwfa.org/

31 Shared with permission; name withheld.

32 Adam Sonfield, Kinsey Hasstedt, Megan L. Kavanaugh, and Ragnar Anderson, *The Social and Economic Benefits of Women's Ability to Determine Whether and When to Have Children* (New York: Guttmacher Institute, 2013), www.guttmacher.org/pubs/social-economic-benefits.pdf.

33 FOX5 News, "Woman Says Christian College Fired Her for Premarital Sex," http://fox5sandiego.com/2013/03/04/woman-alleges-discrimination-against-s-d-christian-college/#axzz2xPEmDXdn.

34 Impolite Company, "The Strange Tale of Teri James and the San Diego 'Christian' College That Fired Her," *Impolite Company* blog, March 2013, http://impolite.co/post/46357494144/teri-james-san-diego-community-college.

35 FOX5 News, "Woman Says Christian College Fired Her for Premarital Sex," http://fox5sandiego.com/2013/03/04/woman-alleges-discrimination-against-s-d-christian-college/#ixzz2xPHCzbF3.

36 Impolite Company, "The Strange Tale of Teri James..."

37 Alan Guttmacher Institute and Physicians for Reproductive Choice, "An Overview of Abortion in the United States," 2003 and 2008.

38 Just in case the craze surrounding *The Prayer of Jabez* by Bruce Wilkinson was before your time, Jabez is mentioned in 1 Chronicles 4:10—"Jabez cried out to the God of Israel, 'Oh, that you would bless me and enlarge my territory! Let your hand be with me, and keep me from harm so that I will be free from pain.' And God granted his request." (www.thejabezprayer.com).

39 Rachel Held Evans, "Privilege and The Pill," *Rachel Held Evans* blog, January 28, 2014, http://rachelheldevans.com/blog/privilege-and-the-pill.

40 Sheryl Sandberg, *Lean In*, 40.

41 Rick Lawrence, *The 2012 Youth Ministry Salary Survey*, *Group Magazine*, http://youthministry.com/files/gr0112_salary_survey.pdf.

[42] President Barack Obama, 2014 State of the Union Address, January 28, 2014, www.whitehouse.gov/the-press-office/2014/01/28/president-barack-obamas-state-union-address.

[43] April L. Diaz, *Redefining the Role of the Youth Worker* (San Diego, California: The Youth Cartel, 2013).

[44] I teach a workshop on how to make "4 Meals in 4 Minutes" and another one about the ministry of the meal table. The first one is a concept I learned by purchasing a ton of yummy food from an online Texas store called Homemade Gourmet (http://shop.homemadegourmet.com/).

[45] Kara Powell and Brad M. Griffin, "The Church Sticking Together: The Vital Role of Intergenerational Relationships in Fostering Sticky Faith," *StickyFaith blog*, http://stickyfaith.org/articles/the-church-sticking-together.

[46] Karol Rose, "What Really Works: Lessons Learned from 25 Years of Workplace Flexibility," Working Mother Media Research Institute, 2010, www.wmmsurveys.com/flexibility.pdf.

[47] Kristen Anderson-Lopez and Robert Lopez, "Let It Go," (Demi Lovato lyrics) *Frozen* (Walt Disney Records, October 21, 2013).

[48] WomenRunners.com, "History of One Racing Woman, Racing Women and Women Having Fun Running," *WomenRunners.com*, www.womenrunners.com/forum_womenhistory.htm.

[49] Runners Connect, "Getting 'Chicked'–A History of Women's Running," *Runners Connect*, http://runnersconnect.net/running-tips/women-runners-then-and-now/.